D0987939

Written
in the
Stars

DEBBIE FRANK

Written *in the* Stars

**Discover the language of the stars
and help your life shine**

DEBBIE FRANK

First published in 2018
by Headline Home
an imprint of Headline Publishing Group

1

J.K. Rowling quote on page 5 from
Harry Potter: A History of Magic (BBC Two, October 2017)
Quote on pages 14–15 from *Astrology, Psychology and the Four Elements*
by Stephen Arroyo © 1975 Stephen Arroyo
Zodiac symbols: MicroOne/Shutterstock

Cataloguing in Publication Data is available from the British Library

Hardback ISBN 978 1 4722 6064 2
eISBN 978 1 4722 6062 8

Typeset in Cormorant by Palimpsest Book Production Limited, Falkirk, Stirlingshire
Printed and bound in Great Britain by Clays Ltd, Elcograf S.p.A.

MIX
Paper from
responsible sources
FSC® C104740

Headline's policy is to use papers that are natural, renewable and
recyclable products and made from wood grown in sustainable forests.
The logging and manufacturing processes are expected to conform
to the environmental regulations of the country of origin.

HEADLINE PUBLISHING GROUP
An Hachette UK Company
Carmelite House
50 Victoria Embankment
London EC4Y 0DZ

www.headline.co.uk
www.hachette.co.uk

To my darling daughter Lulu – you are the star I wish upon.

CONTENTS

FOREWORD: WHAT IS ASTROLOGY?

Astrology is a beautiful, rich language which was first interpreted and spoken by the Ancient Babylonians as early as 5,000 BC. They believed that the movements of the planets were the gods writing messages to mortals in the sky; that these messages, if they decoded them, would open up a dialogue with fate. They began to chart the movements of the planets and stars.

This dialogue continues for us living in the modern day as the universe remains in constant motion and we catch its whisper as it moves. I would say that astrology is actually the mother tongue of life – containing as it does all the insights, symbols and images that reflect life itself. Like any language or body of knowledge it has evolved over time to reflect the changes in society and its idioms.

The renowned 17th century astrologer William Lilly wrote: 'I believe God rules by all his divine providence and that the stars by his permission are instruments.' Today, however, I would describe astrology as being a unique psychological and spiritual tool for uncovering who you are and what gives you meaning in life.

In my own experience, since becoming an astrologer in the mid 1980s, I have found that clients are looking for insights into how to understand themselves and their destiny. How to align with their purpose in this world as well as connect with the right people in love and friendship.

When situations involving love, purpose, wellness or business arise, they can be catalysts that trigger the need for insight into what is going on and why it might be. So my work involves helping mend a broken heart, making a business decision, navigating a dark night of the soul or a transformation that necessitates a change of career. There are many reasons people will consult me but it all boils down to the fundamental search for a sense of meaning, inner peace and insight.

In terms of language and the idea that messages are written in the stars, classical astrology might describe experiences in absolute black-and-white terms, judging certain planetary movements to be either benefic (good) or malefic (bad). Today, we take a more psychological and spiritual approach: I will talk a client through their celestial DNA and their 'star power' so that they can find the meaning in an experience and discover a realm of possible outcomes that transcend labelling as good or bad. As we know, often what seems like a stroke of luck turns out to contain hidden difficulties, and what we initially see as a crisis is laden with opportunities to develop our resilience, power and self-worth.

I hope this book will open up a gateway to the language of the stars so you can enjoy it, speak it, take comfort and guidance from it, and ultimately live it.

INTRODUCTION

Every atom in our body is created by the stars.
Deepak Chopra

The earliest astronomers took note of cycles and recognised that the movement of the planets correlated to events here on Earth. Knowing when the river Nile would flood according to celestial phenomena was vital for crop plantation. The pyramids and underground temples built by ancient civilisations in Egypt and China were specifically aligned with the stars in order to receive their energy. Events on Earth were seen as a direct mirror of celestial events.

The 1st-century Greek philosopher Plato formed this theory of 'as above, so below' in his book *Timaeus*, which considered the universe to be a great living body. He believed the cosmos had the answers to life. His thinking became the basis for hermetic philosophy, a blend of science, alchemy and astrology, and the basis for the development of Western medicine up until after the Renaissance.

Consider for a moment how the external world dominates us today, how we are bombarded with digital media and newsfeeds. Remembering the universal forces removes the massive hype and influence of what's current in our world so we can reconnect with the power within and stabilise the inner self.

WHAT IS WRITTEN IN THE STARS?

So let's get up to date with today's take on what astrology is: the meaning of those messages in the stars! Astrology is both observational and metaphysical. It is multi-dimensional and provides amazing insights if we are able to see the connections, correlations and associations in its images and language and how they play out in our lives. The planets, cycles, orbits and time describe the rhythms of life and life processes. Deepak Chopra notes that we are constantly being sent messages by the universe; we do not experience random occurrences in a chaotic universe but the universe itself is a field of infinite intelligence. He goes on to describe how we are completely immersed in a web of coincidences and synchronicities that guide our *dharma*, or purpose.

As with any language, when considering astrology, it is not about whether you believe in it – just as it's not possible to not believe in Russian – but whether you can speak it! You don't even have to be fluent in astrology to see connections. For example, doctors have reported increased bleeding in surgery during the Full Moon. Yet, study the language more and you get to decipher its fascinating meanings.

If you can read what's written in the stars you will begin to understand the life themes in your chart, which in turn will give you the inside code as to why you are here, your life themes and soul purpose, why things repeat and how you can transform them.

THE MAGIC OF THE UNIVERSE

'I don't think everyone should believe in magic, but I'm not
sure I would trust anyone who doesn't in some way or another'
J.K. Rowling

Astrology does border the realm of magic, even though its astro-
nomical roots are pure science. As the popularity of the Harry
Potter series of books shows, people are looking for magic in their
lives to offset the mundane, the ordinary, the meaningless. The
universe itself is magical with its cosmic energies of nebulae,
galaxies, black holes, fixed stars, constellations and planets.

The esoteric definition of magic is a direct intervention on the
physical body and world by the astral body and world. If we
therefore view astrology as a tool of magic and healing power and
use it consciously and spiritually we can open up the cosmos in
a person's life.

Many people think astrology is about predicting the future, but
in essence it is guidance for understanding and integrating both the
past, present and future. Astrology can be used to measure when and
how certain experiences and life events caused a person to become
stressed or imbalanced in the mind, body or spirit and in retrospect
it is possible to go back over time to discover the cosmic forces of
that period and their meaning, so that the past can be reviewed,
understood from a new angle and healed.

So are you a person who believes in magic or are you a muggle?
Astrology calls us out on our capacity to believe in intangible
forces as real. Sceptics live in one side of their brain, the linear

right brain, and can act as if they are terrified there might be something outside of their control. Personally, I think there is a crisis of belief in our time – there are those who find it impossible to believe in anything outside of the material world, priding themselves on their 'realism'. What they mean is that their linear version of reality must not be questioned.

Yet there is no industry standard for reality, no one size fits all! Reality is individually created by each person, so to dismiss another person's reality because it is incomprehensible to you is intolerance.

UNIVERSAL INTELLIGENCE

The wisdom of the cosmos is available to anyone who wishes to be open to it. However, it's really a denial of your own power if you desire your astrologer or anyone else for that matter to make choices for you. Astrology doesn't give you an excuse for your behaviour. As Shakespeare said: 'The fault . . . is not in our stars but in ourselves.' What's written in the stars can be a conduit to self-empowerment and making enlightened choices.

UNDERSTANDING THE TWELVE SUN SIGNS

Everyone is born under a Sun sign or sign of the zodiac. Your Sun sign lights you like the Sun god Ra, from within. It is the animating force that makes you who you are – instantly recognisable to others. The neat-nick Virgo, the globe-trotting Sagittarian, the chatterbox Gemini. The Sun is our essence – it might be covered over or luminously expressive but it is always our default setting. The Sun sign is a huge indicator of your character, qualities, preferences and patterns. It shows you what kind of journey you're on, your 'best bits' and blind spots. Your helpers, your challenges and weaknesses, and your superpowers.

Knowing more about what makes your Sun sign tick and how this fits into the energy matrix made up of all twelve signs will give you an advantage on the path ahead, what to expect, how to deal with people, how to find your tribe and most importantly who will fire you up in the relationship stakes.

Astrology is a labyrinth of exploration but just through the Sun sign alone we can know so much about a person. We can see how someone might deal with certain experiences or approach the challenges and intricacies of life differently to a partner or work colleague, how they attract this person and not that one. As the cosmos is a field of resonance, certain people on your frequency will be drawn to you and your energy and others will not. I want to help you understand who the best people are for your Sun sign, who to surround yourself with and who is on a different wavelength.

MITIGATING CIRCUMSTANCES!

Usually it's possible to instantly recognise yourself as your Sun sign. However, astrology is far more complex than the Sun signs alone. When you have your full natal chart or birth chart drawn up for the exact time, date and place of your birth then you will see where the Moon, Venus, Mars and all ten heavenly bodies lie, and this builds up more layers to your picture. There are also the angles to consider, your 'rising sign' and the house placements of the planets. You will always be your Sun sign at core but if for instance you are an Aries with Moon in Pisces and Cancer rising, you are going to be a softer version of the go-getting ram. Just saying!

HOW TO USE THIS BOOK AS A LIFESTYLE GUIDE

For my astrological guidance, first read about the four elements of Fire, Earth, Air and Water on page 13 to determine which you fall under and what this means. The elements alone are extremely helpful for giving pointers as to what matters to you and to show your energy blueprint. You'll also get an idea of how your Sun sign element will react to others – will they float your boat, will they be mutually supportive or are you coming from entirely different places? Then turn to the section on your Sun sign for greater insight into the type of person you are, the real you both inside and out. You'll find out what you need for optimum wellness in mind, body and spirit; what kinds of people or scenarios enhance or cramp your style; what life lessons you're here to learn and what you're bringing to the world. Also you'll get the astrological third eye into what you're really looking for in love and relationships, who you should be connecting to and what it takes to capture your interest, keep you and hold you. Even how things come apart! For each Sun sign you'll discover your underlying magnetic attraction and looking up other people's signs will give you the inside track on them – extremely valuable whether you are thinking of having a relationship with them or are already in it as you can avoid the pitfalls. My section on your tribe will reveal what draws you to others in friendship or at work. All these star insights will help you realise your 'star power' as you go through your day-to-day life.

I hope that by gaining some astro-knowledge about yourself it will really help you to shine as you continue on your unique journey through life.

I have also included some guidance in each section by suggesting the best mantra for you to live your life by, the scents that will uplift you, and the objects that you should hold on to and keep close by for the positive energies they emit.

Open your heart to the stars and their messages will set you on course for life.

The ancient language of the stars and planets provides us with keys to understanding exactly who we are, what we are here to learn and how we can live our best lives, no matter how many changes are written into the script.

Essential Energy of the Sun Signs According to Nature and the Seasons

The circle of the zodiac in astrology starts with Aries, the first sign at the spring equinox, distributing the zodiac Sun signs across the constellations in twelve equal parts until we get to Pisces, the final sign.

Aries: spring equinox – birth, libido, growth
(22 March–21 April)

Taurus: cultivating, lush, blossoming
(22 April–22 May)

Gemini: dispersing, changing, pollinating
(23 May–22 June)

Cancer: summer solstice, fullness
(23 June–23 July)

Leo: bright, zenith, playtime
(24 July–23 August)

Virgo: harvest, sifting wheat from chaff
(24 August–23 September)

Libra: autumn equinox, equal day and night
(24 September–22 October)

Scorpio: falling leaves, going within
(23 October–22 November)

Sagittarius: inner light in the dark
(23 November–22 December)

Capricorn: winter solstice, from dark to light
(23 December–20 January)

Aquarius: vision of the future
(21 January–20 February)

Pisces: numinous, mystical, invisible inspiration
(21 February–21 March)

Of course, there is the issue of being born on 'the cusp' as the Sun enters each sign at a different time each year. For ease of use, the approximate times are given above. However, if you were born close to the cusp then it is important to check out your Sun sign according to your exact time, date and place of birth. Your birth chart is available for free on www.astro.com.

THE ELEMENTS:
THE ENERGY OF YOUR
YOU-NIVERSE

FIRE: Aries, Leo, Sagittarius
EARTH: Taurus, Virgo, Capricorn
AIR: Gemini, Libra, Aquarius
WATER: Cancer, Scorpio, Pisces

Are you a bright light (Fire)
An Earth angel (Earth)
A messenger (Air)
An empath (Water)

In a very simple way, the element of your Sun sign shows your essence, the fundamental ingredients of who you are and what means the most to you. Your element shows how you perceive and experience your own reality and also what you put out into your energy field.

Very often the first thing that people notice about you is whether you belong to Fire, Earth, Air or Water. What they instantly pick up on is whether you seem dynamic (Fire), reliable (Earth), mentally curious (Air) or sensitive (Water). Fire crackles with confidence and is eager to move forward; Earth will appear solid, stable and practical; Air will engage you with talk; Water will 'read' you and try to establish emotional connection between you.

Fire, Earth, Air and Water are the primordial building blocks of our nature and universe. They each hold different energies and positions and they translate into very different concepts of reality. In other words, what is real, what matters to Fire signs – activity and progress – is not what means the most to Earth signs, who crave stability and security. Just taking this on board creates a huge shift in terms of understanding where other people are coming from and what makes them tick.

If we can see the world through their eyes, we can make an adjustment. Someone is not being difficult when they insist on rationality (Air) or take everything literally (Earth) or are impatient (Fire) or take everything personally (Water). It's hard for people to jump outside of their pattern of how they relate to the world and other people.

Fire needs to do
Earth needs to build
Air needs to think
Water needs to feel connected

This is the non-negotiable part of our nature. If we don't get enough of what we need, if our environment, our lives or relationships do not reflect our essential requirements, our vital forces, then we are quite literally 'out of our element'. This place, this situation, this person is 'not our thing' and makes us uncomfortable. As Stephen Arroyo describes in *Astrology, Psychology and the Four Elements*: 'In modern physics: earth is solid; water liquid; air gaseous; and fire . . . radiant ionised energy.' These chemical compositions are alive and kicking inside us and we each have one as our primary function. We do, in fact, hold all four elements within our natal birth charts, but our Sun sign reveals the one with which we are most aligned, the one we most identify with, the one that is our comfort zone, our default setting.

However, the elements don't just reflect our physical chemistry but also the esoteric subtle body with which we connect most readily. So the element of Fire is associated with the etheric vital body; Earth with the physical body and senses; Air with the thought plane and mental body; Water with the emotional and astral body.

ELEMENTS AND OUR LIFE FORCE

The ancient Greek philosophy of Aristotle and Plato became the medical model of medieval and Renaissance thinking, which was aligned with man's four essential elements: moral (Fire), physical (Earth), intellectual (Air) and aesthetic and soul (Water). This became the basis of the four humours described by Hippocrates (born 460 BC), who was known as the Father of Medicine for his medical school in ancient Greece. Hippocrates's work centred on how the blood and bodily fluids of the individual translated into specific behaviours and personalities.

Even today, we take blood in order to read all manner of bodily functions. Some consider our blood type to denote specific types of personality, and some of us even adjust our diet accordingly. The Elizabethan audiences whom Shakespeare wrote for were familiar with the Hippocratic concepts that Shakespeare dropped into his plays, describing characters as choleric (Fire), melancholic (Earth), sanguine (Air) and phlegmatic (Water) type personalities.

Modern medicine has diverged into a linear scientific path in the West, although Indian Ayurvedic medicine has maintained its close alliance between personality and physiology. However, the theory of epigenetics, the 'biology of belief', which has been quantified by cutting-edge neuroscientists, is bringing the two together again, integrating the personality with the body. We are reconsidering this ancient wisdom and, under the watchful gaze of MRI scans, concluding that perhaps Hippocrates and his ancient Greek methodology was right!

ELEMENTS AS CHEMICAL ATTRACTION IN RELATIONSHIPS

It gets really interesting when we look at relationships from the perspective of the elements. When we interact with other people, whether we're in a personal or business relationship, the elements of our Sun signs will come into play. We get to experience the alchemy of the elements merging and we can see beyond pure physics to the direct exchange of life forces. For instance, we might get that sense of fanning the flames when Air meets Fire or of Water being poured into the solid container of Earth . . .

In the arena of relating to others we see exactly how elements can 'rub us up the wrong way' or be harmoniously compatible. The combustible energy exchange between two people is pure alchemy that either lights us up, holds us, restricts us, challenges us or supports us. We are fed or depleted by each other's Sun sign elements.

When we spend time with that person the frequencies of our specific elements mingle and tingle. If we sleep in the same bed as them, our energy fields are merging on the astral plane as we lie next to them. If we are in the office, our chemistry is carried on the airwaves into the space and the energy field of the room, creating clouds of thought forms, power struggles, visions and ego desires.

People talk about 'chemistry' between each other. Elements are just that. They describe the electrical charges and forces that surround each person and, more than that, they describe which one of the Fire, Earth, Air or Water priorities, needs, desires and realities is their 'big thing'. Just grasping this about someone can help lift a whole weight of struggle or misconception. If you can see which element they belong to, then you will understand what's going on for them and between you and what kind of ingredients are in the mix.

THE FIRE SIGNS

ARIES * LEO* SAGITTARIUS

Hot, burning, warming, radiating, outgoing, enthusiastic, confident, activating, energising, fighting, taking the initiative, being enterprising. Fire wants to live in a world of colour, zest and drama, as the hero that conquers all. They have an affinity for spiritual potential, growth and development; they know how to generate something, to make an impact on the world and others. Fire is not interested in maintenance as they have a strong nature of desire. They are seekers, edge pushers, explorers. The known is done and dusted, they are on an endless mission of discovery.

In alchemy, the fire process is 'calcinatio' – the capacity to burn and purge. Fire signs eliminate dross through their force and strength of character. Yet the lesson for Fire is not to burn or damage others with their fiery nature. They possess the gifts of potency and agency.

THE EARTH SIGNS

*TAURUS * VIRGO* CAPRICORN*
Holding, stabilising, secure, solid, tethered, resistant, fixing, organising, practical, structuring, creating order out of chaos, grounded in the physical body and the material realm, down-to-earth, always reality-checking.

The earth signs have an affinity with all the natural beauty and treasures of the earth. They want to sustain and are troubled by any change that may cause things to break. They desire for things to either stay the same or build slowly. Earth likes to trace things from beginning to end. They will look at the threads going back to their roots and along to the probable outcome. Earth is connected to the body, the material world and the base chakra which governs all survival instincts. Earth signs like to have a solid connection to all they hold real – often tangible objects pertaining to the five senses.

The Earth alchemical process is 'coagulation' – that which densifies, solidifies and stabilises. Earth brings wild elements together and is able to contain and hold them. The lesson for Earth is not to cause stagnation – a living death – through holding on too tight, not to imprison or limit others. Earth has the gifts of sustainability and protection.

THE AIR SIGNS

*GEMINI * LIBRA * AQUARIUS*
Cool, curious, thinking, communicating, moving, rational, neutral-ising, social, logical. Air uses reason to generate maps and insights. They play with all the thoughts and reasons why, the reactions, newsfeeds and data. They get caught up in their own mind chatter and constantly read what's in the air on the airwaves. As air is everywhere and infiltrates everything, they possess the gift of mobility. Their association with the throat chakra enables them to verbalise ideas. They have to be 'in the know': reading, hearing, talking about every piece of news, the latest events or information.

The alchemical process associated with the Air signs is 'subli-matio' – where physical activity is transformed into sublime understanding. Air has to learn to synthesise all divergent ideas and thoughts and bring them to a vision that is also grounded and works on a material level.

THE WATER SIGNS

*CANCER * SCORPIO * PISCES*
Flowing, feeling, compassionate, connecting, empathising, emotionally intelligent, receptive, sensitive, soothing, giver of solace, replenishing, nurturing. Water seeks to bond and merge. The element of Water is responsive and receiving of other ener-gies and also surrenders to the flow, yet has a power of its own that can be as torrential as a downpour or as still as a tranquil

lake. Water changes shape according to its environment. It has healing properties. The eminent Japanese Doctor Emoto discovered that water itself contains emotionally intelligent memory that reflects thoughts and deeds. Water corresponds to what is swishing around inside of people – the unconscious, subconscious feelings that reside within.

The alchemical process corresponding to Water is 'solution' – the dissolving property that causes solid shapes to release. Water has to master feelings so that they can be contained, yet add depth to words and actions.

COMPATIBLE ELEMENTS

The elements can complement and combine with each other to create mutual growth and support.

In Our Element

If your Sun sign belongs to the same element as another person then broadly speaking you are singing off the same hymn sheet! There will be a sense of desiring similar things, moving through life in similar ways and being with a kindred spirit. Being of the same element immediately provides a strong connection.

FIRE (Aries, Leo, Sagittarius) meets AIR (Gemini, Libra, Aquarius)

These are both yang, extrovert, active, masculine energies associated with outpouring. The doers meet the thinkers. Both these elements aspire to bringing something abstract into being – to express a spark of desire, or a glimmer of an idea. It's the combination of doing and talking. Together they can ramp each other up, turn an idea into an action and spread the word or the energy and enthusiasm. Air and Fire can whip up a storm!

EARTH (Taurus, Virgo, Capricorn) meets WATER (Cancer, Scorpio, Pisces)

These are both yin, introvert, passive, feminine energies associated with sustaining.

Earth and Water are both substantive, concerned with holding things together, understanding things and making them real. Together they can build a relationship or an empire. Earth provides the glue to make things stick and Water is the perceptive, creative outpouring that Earth contains. Earth and Water combine to form a vessel that holds the emotional side of the relationship.

Out Of Our Element
Incompatibility from an element point of view can be challenging, but also exciting and dynamic. We simply need to be more aware of what is important to the other person's energy field.

FIRE (ARIES, LEO, SAGITTARIUS) MEETS WATER (CANCER, SCORPIO, PISCES)

Water can cool fire down, or put it out. Fire wants to do, Water wants to reflect. This can be a romantic and creative combination, or it can be challenging: Fire gets impatient with Water's change-able feelings and Water feels misunderstood and railroaded into doing instead of being. Fire can warm up water, bringing it to a simmer – it's all a question of temperature with this combination, which needs constant adjustment on both sides if it is to work!

FIRE (ARIES, LEO, SAGITTAIURS) MEETS EARTH (TAURUS, VIRGO, CAPRICORN)

Fire can burn through earth, scorching it. Fire is in a hurry, Earth is naturally cautious. This can be a case of opposites attracting and providing mutual benefit or a case of never the twain shall meet. Fire can feel thwarted by the conservative nature of Earth. Earth can tire of Fire's endless quest to move on instead of staying put. Earth can feel very heavy and dense for the Fire person, whilst Fire presents as a challenging child to the Earth person who wants to settle and stabilise. Fire can feel trapped by Earth, a little stifled when Earth can't help pointing out practicalities, which can deflate the grand designs of Fire. However, if they can combine their talents and energies, they can produce something real as well as exciting!

AIR (GEMINI, LIBRA, AQUARIUS) MEETS EARTH (TAURUS, VIRGO, CAPRICORN)

Air wants to fly, to occupy the spaces in between and to cover vast distances. Earth wants to put down roots. This can work well if two people can maintain their own roles. However, Earth can clip the wings of Air, causing them to crash land, and Earth can feel ruffled by Air's inconsistency and constant desire for movement. Earth ties Air down and feels heavy whilst Air lifts Earth up or causes earthquakes! It can be a pull of opposing forces that either changes both for the better or becomes bothersome for both of them!

AIR (GEMINI, LIBRA, AQUARIUS) MEETS WATER (CANCER, SCORPIO, PISCES)

Air want to spread ideas, socialise and be free. Water wants to connect, belong and understand. This combination can work well if both people value what the other has to offer in terms of differentness to their own energy. Yet Air can get weighed down by Water's desire to go deeper. Water meanwhile feels misunderstood and undermined by Air's insistence on rationality when emotional intelligence and feelings are the only litmus test that feels real for Water.

METAPHORS AND SYMBOLS FOR THE SIGNS IN RELATIONSHIP WITH EACH OTHER INSPIRED BY THE ELEMENTS

It's fun to play around with phrases and symbols that describe the union between two signs according to their element! Of course, in the universe it is possible to make any combination work, or to come unstuck with seemingly compatible energies. You can dream up some of your own . . .

ARIES WITH ARIES – fire burns bright
ARIES WITH TAURUS – a slow burn
ARIES WITH GEMINI – Catherine wheel spins in all directions
ARIES WITH CANCER – a shooting star falls into the sea
ARIES WITH LEO – sunshine
ARIES WITH VIRGO – burning man
ARIES WITH LIBRA – a cool breeze on a hot day
ARIES WITH SCORPIO – getting your fingers burned
ARIES WITH SAGITTARIUS – Rocket Man
ARIES WITH CAPRICORN – Stop/go sign
ARIES WITH AQUARIUS – boiling point and cooling down
ARIES WITH PISCES – fire extinguisher

LEO WITH TAURUS – taming the tiger
LEO WITH GEMINI – sparks fly
LEO WITH CANCER – a damp squib
LEO WITH LEO – fire dance

LEO WITH VIRGO – fire screen
LEO WITH LIBRA – fan the flames
LEO WITH SCORPIO – passion burns out of control
LEO WITH SAGITTARIUS – on fire
LEO WITH CAPRICORN – fire drill
LEO WITH AQUARIUS – set alight
LEO WITH PISCES – hot shower

SAGITTARIUS WITH TAURUS – quick, quick, slow
SAGITTARIUS WITH GEMINI – jumping jack
SAGITTARIUS WITH CANCER – fire pit
SAGITTARIUS WITH LEO – lit up
SAGITTARIUS WITH VIRGO – controlled explosion
SAGITTARIUS WITH LIBRA – glow by candlelight
SAGITTARIUS WITH SCORPIO – liquid sunshine
SAGITTARIUS WITH SAGITTARIUS – let's go places
SAGITTARIUS WITH CAPRICORN – no fires allowed
SAGITTARIUS WITH AQUARIUS – lazer light show
SAGITTARIUS WITH PISCES – rain stopped play

TAURUS WITH TAURUS – together forever
TAURUS WITH GEMINI – a kite is controlled by hand
TAURUS WITH CANCER – they hold each other tight
TAURUS WITH LEO – yes you will, no you won't
TAURUS WITH VIRGO – gently does it
TAURUS WITH LIBRA – graceful and slow
TAURUS WITH SCORPIO – the running of the bulls
TAURUS WITH SAGITTARIUS – no – YES
TAURUS WITH CAPRICORN – they planned it for years

TAURUS WITH AQUARIUS – lightning strike
TAURUS WITH PISCES – a sugar cube dissolves

VIRGO WITH GEMINI – they can't stop talking
VIRGO WITH CANCER – exquisitely put together
VIRGO WITH LEO – nothing is ever good enough
VIRGO WITH VIRGO – precision tools
VIRGO WITH LIBRA – perfectly blended
VIRGO WITH SCORPIO – the investigation continues
VIRGO WITH SAGITTARIUS – extra effort is required
VIRGO WITH CAPRICORN – let's make this last
VIRGO WITH AQUARIUS – how can we help?
VIRGO WITH PISCES – the mop meets the mess

CAPRICORN WITH GEMINI – can't make the leap
CAPRICORN WITH CANCER – I will take care of you
CAPRICORN WITH LEO – stop exaggerating
CAPRICORN WITH LIBRA – they have an old-fashioned style
CAPRICORN WITH SCORPIO – so deep with a mysterious
    attraction
CAPRICORN WITH CAPRICORN – they plan to grow old
    together
CAPRICORN WITH AQUARIUS – something old, something
    new
CAPRICORN WITH PISCES – a port in a storm

GEMINI WITH GEMINI – there are four of them in this
    relationship
GEMINI WITH CANCER – be quiet or I'll cry

GEMINI WITH LIBRA – it's a merry dance
GEMINI WITH SCORPIO – the light aircraft meets turbulence
GEMINI WITH AQUARIUS – hippie, hippie shake
GEMINI WITH PISCES – like spinning tops they whirl and twirl

LIBRA WITH CANCER – hearts and flowers
LIBRA WITH LIBRA – they are the original golden couple
LIBRA WITH SCORPIO – the scales shake
LIBRA WITH AQUARIUS – a gentle breeze turns into a
    flurry
LIBRA WITH PISCES – the poolside glamour party

CANCER WITH CANCER   we are family
CANCER WITH SCORPIO – ahh, someone who understands
    me
CANCER WITH AQUARIUS – weird and wonderful or
    worlds apart
CANCER WITH PISCES – dream a little dream

SCORPIO WITH SCORPIO – it's so intense, the passion, the
    intrigue
SCORPIO WITH PISCES – the water gets very deep here

AQUARIUS WITH AQUARIUS – they revel in doing it their
    way!
AQUARIUS WITH PISCES – so much love for the world and
    humanity, it's not all about them

PISCES WITH PISCES – a shoal of fish moves as one

Star Secrets of Relationships

WHAT'S YOUR FREQUENCY?

People who love each other or who share interests have matching frequencies. Scientists are now measuring this but perhaps you've always felt those frequencies that bind you to certain people; you don't need a scanner to tell you what your intuitive radar has always known! Yet astrology tells you your frequency – the element of your Sun sign is a whole satellite dish of its own!

ATTRACTING – HOLDING – LETTING GO

How do you catch the attention of the person you're attracted to? What do you talk to them about? If you know the element of their Sun sign, it's pretty simple!

FIRE – What are you doing?
EARTH – What are you working on?
AIR – What's new?
WATER – How are you feeling?

Getting into a relationship is so much easier than getting out of it! For a start, when all those pheromones are fizzing you are less likely to notice if your Aries is too bossy, your Cancer too clingy, or your Aquarian too icy. It's amazing how magnetic attraction can melt all those warning signs that came up on your dashboard, but you were so excited to go somewhere that you didn't realise your relationship would break down halfway through, that it was never going to go the distance.

So what happens when you're ready to sling your Piscean fish back in the water or you're tired of the gyrating Gemini twins? It depends, of course, how long you've been attached. Yet time is immaterial when you consider the impact certain people can have on your life in a few hours, let alone twenty-five years.

The alchemy of getting dumped is just as fascinating (but much more painful) than the alchemy of catching cupid's arrow. The entry and exit points of a relationship are handled very differently by each of the elements.

Aries, Leo and Sagittarius, being **Fire**, tend to rush in where angels fear to tread. Act first, think later is their modus operandi, so things are going to take off very quickly and can burn out overnight (even if that night is indeed twenty-five years after the first one). Fire requires a lot of engagement with the outside world, with their passions and desires, or life goes flat. You have to keep their fire burning. Excitement ignites their spirit and they always want more in order to offset boredom. Your relationship has to be active and engaging. Challenge is preferable to routine with these signs so relationships must sparkle. Fire energy is so combustible that it can light you up then leave you in the dark – like the switch has been flicked. Once Fire decides it wants something or someone else, that's it. It's over. However hurtful this is, at least it's quick.

For the **Earth** signs, Taurus, Virgo and Capricorn, you're looking at the slow appraisal followed by the carefully managed exit strategy. No surprises either way. As Earth signs value the physical realm above all else, of course looks are going to be important to them. Physically seeing each other is also vital for these signs, who can't last long just on phone contact. Seeing and touching is believing when it comes to the Earth form of love. Getting involved with an Earth sign can be a long drawn-out process and equally laborious at the end as Earth ties you in double knots that are difficult to unpick. What the other elements might consider to be a cage, is actually just a parameter, a boundary, a thing of safety for Earth. Time is important to them: they go into relationships for the long haul and like to know the rules and expectations. They don't adapt easily to change and will view a relationship as a safety net which sustains them. Obviously, a Mercurial, changeable relationship is very challenging for this element. You will have plenty of time to consider what you're getting yourself into with Earth and also time to lick your wounds and sort things out afterwards.

If the love bug has struck with an **Air** sign – Gemini, Libra or Aquarius – then you're bound to be part of something larger than your own relationship: that network of people, that shared interest or activity is the framework that draws you together. Air wants to be on the same wavelength as you – everything is about the mind – so you go in talking . . . and if you're lucky, you're still talking at the end, because 'no speaks' is death to an Air sign. People are oxygen for Air signs and there has to be a throughput of ideas, movement and interests or the Air signs are literally suffocated. Air is the people person, but there can be something a little impersonal about their approach as they are capable of cutting off from their basic human instincts and live in their head. For Air, the love relationship can easily mutate into friendship, which either continues to glue you together or spells the end of passion (and the relationship if this is the one thing you value above all else).

Diving into the **Water** element – Cancer, Scorpio or Pisces – requires full immersion right from the beginning. For Water, their inner world is always going to be a whole universe to them. The outer world is understood through their own personal feelings and responses to it rather than observed with reason and detachment. Water is about emotional intimacy and bonding – your emotional rapport and connection is always going to be the most important component in any relationship. You might find yourself in Loch Ness or Niagara Falls – out of your depth or swept away – or with a gentle fountain that constantly refreshes you. It's hard to end a relationship with a Water sign. On an imperceptible level you can still be connected. Your relationship can hang on like a cactus in the desert, having retained enough emotional connection between you to survive withdrawal.

So, I can't promise you this book will ensure every relationship you encounter transpires without a hitch. However, once you start to learn and recognise some of this astro-speak, you're already going to be adding extra bandwidth to your perception of humanity. An ability to laugh at both our own foibles and the annoying way Taurus moves so slowly, Gemini changes direction and Pisces meanders is part of the healing from expecting everyone to be like us! Besides, compatibility is based on personal prefer-ence – and one person's gift is another person's poison. What this book will help you see is what kind of person is the right fit for you. You can look at your own element and Sun sign – which should feel like looking in the mirror. Then take it a step further and start looking up other people. It can be an 'aha' moment when you realise that Leo just needed a little more attention (love), or the Capricorn required more of your time (respect). Who knew?!

ARIES

ARIES

Chase and be Chased

CORE QUALITIES: *forthright, bold, assertive, enterprising, impatient*

Mantra: Today I will walk slowly and think before speaking.

The constellation of Aries: Aries is located in the northern celestial hemisphere between Pisces to the West and Taurus to the East. Its brightest star is Hamal.

Aries will always comes rushing into your life because they are usually in a hurry. They streak across your path in an instant and, like a comet, light your way. Whether you are in the presence of an Aries Warrior Queen or Aries Superhero, their energy signature burns and crackles with life force. This is a 'no time to waste' person and they are so results-oriented that before you know it they have configured a complicated scenario into an answer. It's breathtaking to watch and be around. Of course, they don't suffer fools gladly so keep your mouth shut if you don't have anything worthwhile to contribute. Aries dazzle with their infectious enthusiasm to get things done. They move things forward. Whether you are working with an Aries, personally involved with one or a burns victim from the crossfire, they light up your life in their bright and spectacular style, making a lasting impact – whether they have been around for a reason, a season or a lifetime. The effect they have on you can be something you never forget. Later, you look back and think: if it wasn't for them I never would have made that move, been brave enough to . . .

The brightness of Aries means that inevitably some people will get caught in their headlights. They can crackle with impatience so that you have to make a snap decision, and this is the very thing the Earth and Water signs are afraid of. However, at the risk of getting run over – needs must – those who take a while usually manage to find something in themselves that causes a jump one way or another. For Aries, it only matters that you do SOMETHING – inertia is their bugbear. Unforgivable passivity is considered the ultimate weakness.

LIFE

Health

Aries possess full *chi* – the energy or life force that courses through every cell in their being. They are phenomenally energetic and bouncy and need to 'do' things in order to feel at their most alive. The Aries zest for life is infectious in the best possible way, so you will feel highly charged when you are around them – as if you have plugged yourself into the mains!

Mind

Aries thrives on stimulation and new challenges. They have a low threshold of boredom, preferring to initiate rather than deal with the slog of working things through. Their mental sharpness always spots how to take things forward and the Aries mental mantra is 'never look back'. Aries is able to channel ideas that are flying around in the stratosphere of the mental plane. They are always ahead of the game which gives them genius thinking – they create the zeitgeist rather than go along with it. However, they can't always ground these ideas, getting excited about concepts and moving so quickly to the next one that many are left behind unfinished. The Aries thinking is idealistic and ahead of the curve. When they do manage to anchor the idea and manifest it into reality it can happen at the speed of light.

Body

Aries is ruled by Mars, the red planet, which fuels this energetic Fire sign with desire. Mars rules the head and the ram is famously 'hot headed', both emotionally in terms of being quick to anger and literally as they are prone to inflammatory conditions associated with the head, such as migraine, fever and physical injury.

Ultimately, Aries needs to slow down and cool down in order to avoid burnout. However, if there is not enough action in their lives their frustration levels severely impact their wellbeing.

Spirit
The Aries spirit likes to be stimulated. Boredom and routine crush them and bring out the worst in them. Ideally, they find an avenue in life which will provide them with so much of the new that they can constantly move from one goal to the next, constantly press the refresh button. Aries do not do well if they have no space for their enterprising, entrepreneurial spirit to shine.

As a sign, Aries has an innate capacity to recognise what they desire. This is a gift that keeps them young at heart and engaged with life, but their desires can also trip them up, propelling them towards the quick fix, or instant gratification, rather than the satisfaction of real achievement.

Call it selfish, but certainly Aries incarnates with the necessary drive to establish a core self in the first place. And this is the starting point for relationships, because knowing yourself is a prerequisite to move from an 'I' to an 'us' situation.

Aries is a bold, daring and courageous sign – a kind of one-person start-up. They get things going, they are initiators and provide the impetus for many adventures and projects, not to mention relationships! However, their interest can flag once the initial excitement has worn off. They get bored with practical details and prefer to delegate the little things, the small tasks, whilst focusing on winning big battles and overcoming huge challenges.

Spititually and Karmically

If you believe in karma and reincarnation, then you might consider whether Aries has come into this world with some experience on the battlefield. Their unquestioning capacity to go all out for something they want stems from an unwavering belief in their right to have it.

Undoubtedly, the life path of Aries will involve having to conquer something, to establish their independence and hone their warrior skills. They are born knowing how to fight. Their task in this lifetime is to learn how to settle scores through compromise and acceptance. Aries considers capitulation to another person's point of view a weakness, not seeing the power it bestows on them to act gracefully instead of wilfully. These souls embody alpha energy – both the male and female are tanked up with testosterone that fuels their desire to win at all costs. Their weakness, their shadow, can sometimes be seen in bullying others into submission because they are irritated, and then despising the other person's sensitivity towards their aggression. Tears are a no-no with Aries, they can't stand being around what they perceive as weakness in others, the humiliation of the ego, even if they have caused it. This is because Aries can't bear to think that they too possess weakness.

Aries admires people who can do their own thing without constantly checking in with them to see whether they're doing it right. If you are in a relationship with Aries you are expected to stand on your own two feet, not be a hanger-on. However, Aries has their own often unrecognised weakness, which is feeling crushed by not being seen as superior or strong. Strangely their innate self-confidence and self-belief can be eroded by not being seen, admired or respected by others.

Aries tends to live in a world of duality populated by winners and losers, leaders and followers. Their karmic task in this lifetime is to take a leaf out of Libra's book – their opposite sign – and learn the art of cooperation, negotiation, compromise and acceptance. These things can be the hardest task for Aries but if they can evolve in this way then their fiery spirit is burnished to perfection. If they can master the art of being the strong one who gives in, then a very deep soul lesson is learned.

Eating humble pie and saying sorry is hard for Aries. Their egos are strong and surprisingly fragile at the same time. You have to appeal to their heart and fire-power. However, having an Aries around is like having your champion there 24/7. They will always encourage you to go for it. When you are down they can lift you up with the sheer confidence of their spirit. They believe in themselves and if they believe in you too, there is little you can't achieve together. They will always encourage you to be strong, to take a risk, to go for it. However, they can be so demanding, intimidating and grabby that you wonder if perhaps it's true that the world really does revolve around them. Sharing and compromise are life lessons. If they can stay with what is, rather than what's next, their journey of enlightenment is easier.

What Does Aries Have to Give?
If you are around the ram energy, you will immediately feel the charge of their life force that lights up the room. When Aries arrives, things start to happen! They will buck you up, challenge you to a duel of minds and expect that you give things your best shot.

It is always around an Aries that things get moving, the faint-hearted receive the necessary injection of confidence, the naysayers get rebuked. Think of the energy and life force of spring and the spring equinox, especially as the ultimate symbol of new beginnings. The thrust of the bulb to break open the hard ground of winter is what Aries has to offer.

What Does Aries Need to Receive?

The Aries fire needs to be tempered by those who are calmer and cooler. It is an art to get them to see another point of view without putting out their fire or riling their rage. The trick is never to take their abrasive manner personally and to recognise that Aries thinks on their feet without a filter and therefore how they come across is just sheer force of nature. Besides, after they have attacked you they will forget they even said anything. As Aries is all about heat, much is said in the heat of the moment without forethought. If you can get Aries to see that they have been rash, that there is another way to look at things, then they can quickly back down. The trick is to do it without making them look like a hothead, which Aries sees as an affront to their valour, their self-esteem. They do not want to admit defeat, but they can reconfigure their position and views if presented with a new angle.

What Does Aries Need to Learn?

The ram is so confident of their leadership abilities that this can have the effect of coming across as selfish. The shadow side of their nature in a less evolved Aries always looks after numero uno and considers everyone else to be an also-ran. This only works in single competitive sports, certainly not in the relationship arena. So Aries needs to be the purest form of their fire-power, which looks after others, fights for a cause, starts the fire of passion in other people's hearts and knows how to negotiate, compromise and be considerate towards others. As Aries is so fired up with their initiatives and new beginnings, they often overlook issues such as consequences. An Aries who has turned their desire to conquer the world into conquering their own impetuous nature is the true winner. When the ram can appreciate the value of being as well as doing, of the yin to their yang then their spirit is burnished gold.

LOVE

Dating: Love at First Sight

The ram is a creature of combat and competition, and therefore you will never arouse their attention or desire if you surrender. They adore a moving target, setting their sights on you as you provoke their interest by appearing hard to get. The ram wants you and that means capturing you, winning you over. You are territory, a goal, a love object and they would be prepared to fight for you – fight off other admirers, fight your resistance. Defeat is not a word in the Aries repertoire. The ram wants to overcome the odds, so don't make yourself too available! Whilst other signs would tire of forever chasing, this is the Aries primary attraction factor. Conquest is their forte. The ram can be attracted to another alpha type who exudes the chemistry and confidence to win them over. However, once won they will not settle into playing second in command as the Aries warrior spirit demands either top or equal billing. Aries needs the cut and thrust of everyday battle and if there is not enough in the outside world to engage them then their feisty spirit will pick battles with you in order to feed their hunting instincts.

A beta mate or date is a different ball game. It works as long as you are not too compliant, otherwise you will not pique their interest. In fact, opposing them can be the very thing that enables the love dart to strike.

A relationship with an Aries is not for those who measure love by its serenity! As this sign gets bored by familiarity, even going to the same restaurant twice in a row could be a problem. Aries likes to discover the new, to be the first with the latest and the best. So, if you are dating an Aries, take them to unexplored territory and preferably arrange to 'do' something together rather than just hang out. Most rams get bored to death just chilling and start pacing like a captive tiger.

They're sporty, active and spontaneous, so don't think you can woo Aries with a date planned weeks in advance. Invite your ram on the spur of the moment to go hiking, just because the sun came up this morning, or to the sports event that pulses with adrenaline and you will see their fire burn brighter. The ram isn't one for beating about the bush either. If they like you, you will know about it. Aries can deliver a love arrow straight to your heart in a second and they don't appreciate being kept waiting for a response!

You don't have to be a world leader or corporate head honcho to pique their interest. They just like to know that you are strong – in mind, body and spirit! A well-honed body is a plus, as is a mate who knows their own mind and has a strong spirit that will not be crushed by struggles. Ideally you will be following your passion, doing your own thing, establishing a start-up. Whatever it is you do, make sure you are doing what you love and are not taking the easy option.

When dating, Aries may test you with a few other love interests just to see if you have what it takes. They like to know they are a prize you are willing to fight for. What they despise is indecision. So, if you are dithering over whether this is the one, don't!

The ram needs to be respected for their own achievements and to lead their own lives, even if they are madly in love with you (and there is rarely any other kind of Aries). Even when they test you out by talking about a solo trip to Machu Picchu just when you were planning to take things to the next level, let them do what they need to do – if you really want them, that's the way it has to be. Trying to mould them into something they are not will never work and you will end up with a very unhappy pale imitation of the adventurous ram you fell in love with.

If your idea of love is to be an object of desire then you have got the right sign. The real work is in remaining desirable to them on an everyday basis. Aries comes on strong and fast. They will rush you into a relationship before you have had time to learn their surname, sweeping you off your feet with their ardent need to have you with them – tomorrow, next week, but longer than that and the ram finds it hard to commit! If you are dating a ram then be prepared to live in the now – which spiritually speaking is a very good way to live. Do not try to force any commitment or it will backfire on you, with the emphasis on the fire! Do not send out distress signals when the ram fails to text you back or return your calls. You have to prove you are an independent person who can survive with or without the ram (both are a challenge!).

In the bedroom Aries is easily smitten if there's passion and desire but, of course, their me-first attitude can, on occasion, extend to their lovemaking. However, they are bold and able to express their affections without embarrassment or holding back. You know where you are with Aries. If they fancy you, they want you. It can be very intoxicating to be their object of desire. The real challenge, though, is to keep them interested.

Aries are idealistic in love – they search for the grand romance, the all-encompassing passion that ignites them body, heart and soul. They are not immune to the eyes-across-a-crowded-room scenario; love at first sight comes naturally to them because they are so adept at making quick decisions and knowing how they feel.

To truly fit with an Aries, you have to be your own person,

modelling the fact that you have no need to score every point but remaining challenging enough to keep them on their toes. Of course, whilst Aries is busy rushing around, they need an anchor, a listener, a person who neutralises all the heat and fury in the world out there. If you are looking for excitement and fire, romance and adventure, and appreciate being desired – really desired – then you have met your match. If you don't mind being told what to do and can bask in knowing that you must absolutely be the prize if Aries has expended all that energy in capturing you, then this is a perfect fit.

Keeping . . . Aries on Their Toes in the Long Game
If you have got to the stage of getting your Aries to commit to you then you must have something very special about you. Remember Aries likes winners so you have passed the test! The Aries partner is a handful, no doubt about it, but just as you are getting fed up with their latest enthusiasm they turn their attention back to you and say something drop-dead direct that comes straight from the heart. And that's it, you are conquered again! Of course it's not going to be a smooth ride, mainly because Aries thrives on warfare.

Their default setting is to oppose and challenge so don't expect capitulation, peace and harmony, never mind the bed of roses. Whether you are fighting over which way to make the tea or how to balance the household budget, Aries will always have very strong opinions and will be assertive in delivering them. Even if the contretemps descends into an all-out ambush attack, it will never last very long. At least for Aries. They can trade insults yet the next minute all is forgotten and they are basking in the adrenaline rush whilst you are bandaging your burned fingers. Aries doesn't bear grudges and gives people chances, because they want to be 'engaged' with you. Flatlining into domesticity and routine will kill their passion, so keep sparking their excitement. Your Aries partner needs plenty of space to do their own thing, which doesn't always include you. Give them their own territory, let them lead from the front and you will receive them back into your fold. Do not crush their sense of adventure, or keep them waiting. They are not going to enjoy chilling out with nothing to do at home. They need action so give them a job, a challenge, a spontaneous idea and above all keep those home fires burning because they will want to return to a place of warmth and love.

As Aries is a Mars-ruled sign, it is very hard for the ram to see another person's point of view. Their me-first attitude comes from being the first sign of the zodiac, as the Western zodiac begins at the spring equinox. They consider themselves to be the leader and you are the follower. This is what you signed up for if you marry or live with an Aries. The actual business of give and take doesn't come naturally but can be learned over a period of time, over years of surviving the little skirmishes which come with accommodating another person's needs and wishes. Blazing arguments are often part and parcel of a committed relationship with an Aries, so you need to learn how to give as good as you get. Aries doesn't respect anyone who just submits and will enjoy your company even more if you are able to stand up for yourself. They are dominant, no question about it, but you can learn to live with and love this great human spark, appreciating the zest, warmth and energy of this sign whilst not taking it personally if you are the object of their irritation and fiery temper.

'The Art of War for Lovers' would be the signature anthem for this sign. The Aries passion is ignited by battle. However, if you are to keep the ram you must not get entrapped in the passive-aggressive pattern that surrounds Aries in their encounters with others. Even though they try to make you subservient, to even bully you into submission on occasion, you have to realise that for them this is sport and water off a duck's back. They don't seriously expect you to lie down and take it. Crucially, they will get very bored if you do. You can't afford to fear confrontation with your Aries mate – it would be unwise to constantly give in. Aries wants you to have an opinion, to stimulate and charge the atmosphere with a different take on life. They might not (probably will not) agree with you, but they admire those who have the courage to be themselves.

Honesty is important to Aries. When expressing their thoughts, they can be direct to the point of being rude, because they don't really care what you think. This is why they often don't put solutions out to tender, they just make an announcement of their unilateral decision, their done deal, assuming it is the right one because it is theirs. Often Aries learns the hard way that it is not all about them!

Being pushy and bossy is the way they live their lives, even if it is tempered by Venus in their chart! Besides, if you had wanted someone more polished or laid-back, you wouldn't have chosen an Aries. At least with Aries what you see is what you get and there is no hidden agenda. There is even something quite childlike about their enthusiasm and sense of adventure which of course rubs off on you. If you are in a relationship with an Aries, you will never be bored again. Aggravated, infuriated –

yes! But that is the price you pay for living with this high-energy individual.

Aries can easily attract a lover or end a relationship because beginnings and endings are their forte, but the hard part is making it last. For a start, they get bored rather easily and their lack of sensitivity towards others can endanger even the best relationships.

The Ex Factor: Been There, Done That
If things have gone wrong with an Aries, you might be surprised at the speed with which love hit the skids. No second chances; if you have wounded their ego, that's it. Their revenge is to drop you at lightning speed and it will be over before you know it. Whether you are the breaker or the break-ee, the term 'quickie' divorce must have been invented for Arians.

One of the main reasons for relationships to break down is a lack of passion. Of course over time the initial spark often reduces in a relationship but if you want your Aries partner to continue to want you, then you absolutely must fan the flames of his or her ardour. You can't just settle into the cosy life, because Aries doesn't DO cosy! In fact, it's anathema to this high-flying, highly driven sign. Sexually, things must never become humdrum or their attention could wander elsewhere. Aries are susceptible to instant attraction and their questing, conquering nature could turn temptation into a full-blown affair. Their saving grace is that Arians are not great at keeping more than one fire going, lacking the micro-management skills and being a basically honest sort. If you are smart enough to ensure you are igniting their interest, keeping things alive, new and exciting and that you are also keeping your ram on their toes so that they never become complacent about having 'got' you, then this will be an eternal flame. Allowing them to notice that you remain attractive to others is also key to keeping them on track because their competitive drive will suddenly spring into action. In having to vanquish the competition, your Aries partner will be reminded that YOU are the prize.

Divorcing can be a prime battlefield for the Aries ego to play out in endless rounds of fighting for every last issue. The ram will want to win at all costs, especially if their pride has been hurt in the first place. After the initial swift rejection or separation, the ram will regroup to fight the battle – and never forget that this sign rather enjoys a fight and is also especially good at it.

Of course, you might find that your Aries just wants to move on as quickly as possible. In which case you might not see them for dust. They will ride off into the sunset to chase another adventure without looking back. That can hurt as much as the break-up itself. You can quickly become history with an Aries (who isn't much interested in that subject) because what drives them is the new.

Fairness is not exactly a concept that is on the same frequency as Aries as they are so instinctively attuned to their own needs that there is a blind spot regarding anyone else's. Therefore, in any division of spoils, Aries will want to claim the major part for themselves. However, in certain cases and depending on what went wrong and what other factors they have in their natal chart, Aries can do the big-hearted thing and allow the other person to 'win'. It is a kind of heroic valour that gives them the moral high ground, which is in itself a win for them.

Once a divorce or parting is over and if there are children

involved, Aries often comes into their own as a single parent, stepping up to the plate and making it all work. They enjoy being active parents, ensuring their brood are well equipped to make a go of life and imbuing them with independence and inner strength.

DESTINY

The Aries Team of Conquerers

If you find yourself in any kind of team or group with Aries, you're going to have to up your game. You see, Aries doesn't do losing! You have to be smart, capable of working independently, self-sufficient but also a real team player. The cheer leader is, of course, the ram, who brays loudly from the front, shouting at everyone to keep up, to try harder! Your team must go all out to win, to get the desired result, to be better than all the others. This works so well in competitive sports and in the workplace. On a more social level, when it comes to the pub quiz, the bake-off, the 'friendly' debating team, Aries just can't resist thundering through and vanquishing all opposition!

As a friend, the ram likes to do rather than just be. They will come with you and talk whilst you jog or walk the dog, but sit them down at the kitchen table for a cup of tea and a chat and they'll be twitchy before you know it. The rams don't enjoy aimless conversations. Everything must have a purpose – besides, they are so busy, they simply can't spare the time . . .

Despite all this activity, Aries is a wonderful friend, encouraging and warm. They remind you that the spark of life is very precious.

ARIES

ALTAR OBJECTS

Place some of these objects on your altar or carry them with you in actual or pictorial form.

*

CRYSTAL: diamond, bloodstone, jasper

MINERAL/METAL: iron

ARIES SYMBOLS: the ram or sheep, Mars symbol

TAROT CARD: The Fool

ANGEL CARD: Angel Malahidael, Archangel Ariels

FLOWERS: honeysuckle and thistle

TREE: sandalwood, eucalyptus

SCENTS AND CANDLES: wood, spice or citrus: nutmeg, clove, lemon and grapefruit

MEMORY BOARD/PHOTOGRAPHS/PICTURES: trophies, prizes, Olympic winners, achievements; painting: 'Venus and Mars' by Sandro Botticelli

CLOTH: scarlet red, fine cotton

TALISMAN: Mars, diamond shape, red charm

*

TAURUS

TAURUS

Easy Does It

CORE QUALITIES: *Solid, rooted in material reality, strong desires and attachments*

Mantra: I bend and am flexible in order to free-up my resistance.

The constellation of Taurus: Taurus is a large and prominent constellation in the Northern hemisphere's winter sky. Its brightest star is Aldebaran, the thirteenth brightest in the sky, and Taurus also contains the Pleiades star cluster.

Taurus is the slow burn; it is a rare Taurean who acts on impulse, so when dating a bull, you will have a long time to get to know each other. They have no wish to rush in and they enjoy taking their time to savour the whole business of a relationship. Taurus sets no store by being swept off their feet. On the contrary, their hooves are planted firmly on the ground and woe betide anyone who tries to hurry them into anything before they are ready. They are inherently risk-averse, so each time they see you is another opportunity to gather facts. Yes, facts! Trying to romance a Taurean with mirages and smokescreens will never work. They will remain steadfastly rooted to the spot, and won't move a millimetre closer to you just because you are spinning an extraordinary storyline. Taurus invented the reality-check. So expect to be checked. And checked again! They don't want to make a mistake, you see. So they will watch you, eat with you, walk with you, enjoy any number of activities with you for the sole purpose of seeing if you are consistent, if you really are who you say you are. This is not to say they are going to put the forensics onto you (leave that to Scorpio – their opposite sign). They are perfectly content to just bide their time, put you in different situations and see if you hold together, stack up, if your character is the common denominator. If nine times out of ten they are content in your company and you did nothing to frighten the horses then you are a good person in their books. They can forgive the one transgression because Taurus understands human fallibility, but doesn't want to experience it too often.

LIFE

Health

Taurus is the sign of abundance. They look as though they have just arrived from the Garden of Eden via a golden glow day at the spa. If contentment is the elixir of health and happiness, then Taurus knows how to bottle it and their sensual appreciation of life lights up their aura. Taurus may overdo the earthly pleasures a little, but they tend to have a rock-strong constitution, withstanding stress that would floor other signs.

Mind

Taurus likes to digest concepts slowly and they learn thoroughly at their own speed. Inherently literal and practical it is hard for them to grasp the intangible. They simply don't believe in anything that can't be measured or held. Nuance and free association do not come naturally to this sign, which takes things as they are, not as they could be. Essentially practical and having so much common sense, they get irritated by those who take off on flights of fancy. The Taurean world is on the vibration of the third dimension, meaning that it is quite dense and solid, revolving around material objects and linear thinking. Taurus doesn't do hidden meaning, preferring to deal with the obvious rather than the obtuse. The caricature Taurean mentality is if you can't touch, see, smell, hear or preferably eat it then it doesn't exist. The more subtle and elevated dimensions are a realm that many Taureans are afraid of, yet if they dare to open their minds to look inside they would find riches beyond their dreams.

Their thinking is built on what has worked before, so their

knowledge stems from history rather than ingenuity. Their motto is 'why reinvent the wheel'.

Body

Luscious and sensual, their magnetic physicality exudes the message that the body is their temple. You might come across the heavenly Aphrodite type, or the Love God – or, if Taurus has given in to too many physical temptations and indulgences combined with a penchant for a life of ease, you sometimes see the super-sized and somewhat ample but still winsome looking Taurus. Taurus enjoys pampering the body and all the creature comforts that appeal to their senses.

Food is a number-one priority and most Taureans will go to great lengths to ensure that eating is a pleasurable experience. Taurus rules the neck and the throat and most have beautiful, resonantly velvet voices.

Taurus possesses enormous powers of endurance and their capacity to cling on can translate into retention of fluids and waste products in the body. They need to learn to let go and break the habit of accumulation that can become endemic in every cell of their being.

Spirit

Taurus is all about attachment. In fact, there is nothing casual about Taurus, who has a strong need to attach to and possess whatever they desire. They are the master builders of the zodiac and they will diligently work to sustain, preserve and contain whatever is important to them. They have a gift for manifesting and for prosperity as they understand the laws of the physical universe. Even the less-than-flush Taurean is a person who appreciates and is grateful for the simple pleasures in life, which in turn increases their capacity to attract more of what they value . . .

Spiritually and Karmically

Taureans are here to engage with the physical realm, immersing themselves in managing, securing and making safe. They have an innate affinity with nature and the land, understanding the cycles, rhythms and seasons of life. It seems they are born with this knowledge. Many Taureans have green fingers but their nurturing skills can work equal wonders on humans.

Whilst others flounder, give up and get lost, Taurus plods along, knowing the wisdom of the saying 'when the going gets tough, the tough get going'; they are the tortoise, not the hare. Taurus will stick things out, keep at it and usually get there in the end. Disliking chopping and changing, this sign will enjoy a long-lasting career, still in the same job years after others have moved on. They are associated with making things last.

In this lifetime, Taurus is imbued with a huge survival instinct. They are calm in a crisis and know how to find and give shelter to those who are vulnerable. Their strength and poise is much sought after, especially by those who need a role model for standing firm, not letting things get to them and holding their ground.

Whilst Taurus exudes stoic energy, they tend to despise what they perceive as lack of self-control or sense. Of course, as opposites tend to attract, they can magnetise people who wilt at the first problem, dither and cause chaos. Their karmic lesson is to learn the value of feelings and all that lies in the realm of the subconscious or that which can't be explained. Taurus mistrusts and fears anything that threatens to overwhelm their world of order, not realising that this place of mystery is the crucible of creativity. Whilst they themselves are masters of constancy and everything which is everyday, they must make room for the occasional and extracurricular. If they can go deeper, explore questions that do not have a practical answer then they add volume to their vocabulary, insight to their building blocks.

What Does Taurus Have to Give?
If you are around a Taurus, you will blossom under their steady nurturing gaze. Taurus is associated with fertility and there is a peculiar optimum environment that they create which enables others to flourish. Of course, if you are an impatient, restless type, you may not want to hang around long enough to receive their steady drip-drip watering system. You may interpret the safety and comfort zone that is created by Taurus as a place of stagnation and claustrophobia where nothing ever changes. If you prefer danger and the excitement of not knowing what's going to happen next, then Taurus is not for you. The comfort of predictability is for those who need an anchor.

What Does Taurus Need to Receive?
Taurus as an Earth sign is about establishing the lay of the land. However, there are times when this sign benefits from the Earth moving! They resist change, which is a word this sign dreads to think about. Yet change can be a wonderful thing and brings fresh

life, new angles and ideas into a world that has become so climate-controlled that nothing new enters or emerges. If Taurus can receive some level of upheaval into their lives, they usually benefit in the end – if you can get Taurus to see that never changing is stifling, that just because it's the way it's always been doesn't make it right or better.

What Does Taurus Need to Learn?

Taurus is easily the most stubborn sign of the zodiac. It is their way or the highway, but delivered with such inimitable charm your satnav automatically changes! Their propensity for acting as the immoveable object can drive most other signs to the brink of madness. Their force of resistance is immense. They can make life very hard both for themselves and for other people with their unbending attitude, and the fact that they are always right 'just because', no question.

In the end, things take longer and waste time and energy if Taurus cannot find some flexibility. However, the bull hopes that by digging in their hooves they will wear you down. The other shadow side of their nature is the raging bull, which can charge in a terrifying manner if their patience has been exhausted. It takes a lot to rile a Taurus but they are dangerous if they get to that stage. If you venture into Taurus territory you are dealing with an essentially female sign that translates into a strong female and male energy.

The Taurus may be accused of overly simplifying matters because they like the simple life. But if you hang out with Taurus long enough, you will see the contrasts and contours that are inherent in the bull. They are passive, laid-back and restful yet literally possess the stamina of an ox. They are masters of both attachment and resistance, pulling in, holding tight so that whatever is close remains close, and resolutely pushing away what is undesirable to them.

LOVE

Dating: the Law of Attraction

In order to attract a Taurus you need to look good. These Venus-ruled people appreciate beauty and physical charm. At the very least you must be comfortable in your body, in your own skin. This ticks another Taurean box. A fundamental prerequisite is that you know how to relax, as Taurus is the opposite of the uptight, nervous control freak and favours those with whom chilling out is easy and comfortable. If you have a problem with enjoying being lazy and indolent at times, then Taurus will have a problem with you!

Apart from that you should appreciate the good things in life – which to Taurus amount to good-quality food, beautiful things that appeal to the senses, textures, scents and sounds, pleasing surroundings, nature in its bounty and, of course, affection, presence and an unhurried smoothness. In short, Taurus is a lover of all that is luscious, sometimes luxurious and certainly indulgent. Therefore, you will not impress if you date them 'on the hoof', unplanned, taking pot luck, making it up as you go along – this is not the way to win a Taurean heart. Neither is a cheapskate date – not because Taurus is a gold-digger, but they just equate their own self-worth with being worth it to others.

Unless you have formally asked them out, itemised where you are going and confirmed it in writing, Taurus feels uncertain and a little adrift. The bull doesn't do spontaneity as it could interfere with quality control – and quality is essential and preferable to surprise and excitement! If you are being taken out by a Taurus, they will book both you and the venue in advance and take you to one of their favourite tried-and-tested places so that nothing can go wrong. If you don't enjoy eating, things could get a little tricky.

Taureans, despite their sensual nature which can't help touching and showing affection, will usually take things slowly. They are physically sensual, but the initial appreciation is through the eyes as they take you in. (Most probably you will be doing the same, as Taurus tends to be either an earth goddess or nymph or a perfectly formed Adonis). Taurus is not a fast mover, they like to build a relationship slowly, brick by brick. In fact, you are an investment to them, whether they are spending money on you or investing their heart; they will not do either of these things lightly.

The energetic vibe you get from Taurus is basically very appealing and also safe. Yes! They somehow transmit a kind of rock-like quality, so even if they look like a total babe, all dewy, springy and succulent, their energy is steady and you'll want to snuggle into it.

Taurus has such a strong physical presence that you can't help wanting to get close, primarily because their physical magnetism is so powerful. They have so much Earth energy in their aura, like a heavily laden double-blossom cherry tree. If a Taurus takes you in their arms, the hold you get is probably the most comforting, reassuring hug you've had since you were in nappies. It's all part of their charm and many signs immediately fall into this embrace, which caresses and enchants them into thinking nothing can possibly go wrong in their lives again. It is the 'I will take care of you' Taurean vibration that is transmitted through your body straight into your heart. They literally ooze safety.

If you are wooing a Taurean, make sure you're right there with the creature comforts. So not somewhere lacking in basic amenities, and if in nature (a bucolic setting is a great aphrodisiac for this sign) at the very least a picnic rug and a hamper of goodies. Touch is the second language of Taurus, so don't hold back on the affection. Taurus will notice the feel of your hand, the texture of your skin and hair, the length of your eyelashes. Your smell is also of paramount importance – a primitive bodily scent can arouse Taurus as easily as an expensive perfume.

To further attract the interest of this sign you must be confident, to know what you are doing. Do not be some flaky, soft-brained type filled with flashy fantasies of unachievable dreams. Preferably you have got some experience under your belt, have a proven track record. You function well on planet Earth. Taurus likes to look after people, but there is a limit to how attractive you seem to Taurus if you really can't get your act together. Taurus is a sign of substance and you need to be fully formed and functioning to be of value to them. Yes, at the heart of the matter when dating Taurus is the fact that they need to be able to cultivate you. To bring out the best in you. But at the very least, all the seeds need to be planted before they will pick up their trowel.

Keeping things simple works best when dating a Taurus as they detest complications. So if you are the type who likes to play games, if romance is about intrigue and mystery for you, then you are barking up the wrong bull here. Taurus is inherently straightforward and 1 + 1 = 2. They also respond happily to the simple things in life, which is a virtue – the aroma of good coffee, the smell of freshly cut grass, a good book, a good movie, holding hands, an arm across their shoulder and, of course, amazingly delicious food – which is the straightest arrow to their heart and works every time.

Keeping: to Have and to Hold

Taurus is a keeper. No doubt about it. They're not into meaningless flings because they can't stand change. Making adjustments is a problem for them so, unromantic as it sounds, when Taurus gives their heart it is so much easier to leave it where it is.

If you want to bag a Taurus, be prepared to wait patiently. Taurus believes that anything worth having is worth waiting for. They mistrust anything that arrives too quickly. There is a process, a procedure to follow, that is slightly different for each and every Taurus but nevertheless has to be followed to the letter. Love for them must be real. Their version of reality is solid and dependable. You must be who you say you are, turn up when you say you will, be prepared to plan things months in advance. Let-downs and flimsy excuses will not wash with Taurus as they mean you are not for real . . .

So let's say you are now happily ensconced with a Taurus. Happily, because who wouldn't want to be enveloped in their care and comfort zone? And if you weren't happy, then you would have exited the stage long ago. You have finally got to the commitment stage. And commitment is a word that Taurus understands through and through. They know the meaning of being with someone when the chips are down, through thick and thin, for better or worse. They are your stalwart companion, always there for you. You are now in this for the long haul. Taurus will weather any storm, defiantly cutting through any turbulence with their failsafe routines and dependable structures. In fact, they have a knack of making you feel that problems are not as big as you imagined. There's nothing that can't be solved with a cup of tea! Just being around Taurus with their unruffled nature, means that dramas must not be allowed to overtake the pecking order of their daily lives. As long as you have a good night's sleep then any calamity can be dealt with in Taurus's books.

This is fine if you like being soothed, but for some partners it is infuriating that their issues are being seen just as a minor inconvenience and not in full, glorious technicolour. The Fire signs like to embellish the dramas of life, for instance, and can begin to feel that their experiences are not being seen and heard or given credence. The Taurus reductionist method can create a sense of alienation for those who thrive on life's ups and downs. It can even feel like a flatline of boredom. The Taurus capacity to 'not go there' inevitably means that much of life is left unacknowledged. Just because Taurus does not wish to visit the realm of anxiety, mystery or curiosity does not mean that others are satisfied being denied a visa.

Once you are firmly embedded with your bull it is important to remember that they have ownership rights on you. Taurus is a sign of attachment that runs so deep, you feel you have signed up for not just this life, but all lifetimes across time and space. You are Theirs, they are Yours. Pretty soon you could feel like a possession – a prized one, but nevertheless an object of their material reality that unequivocally belongs to them. In long-term relationships this can create a safety net that ensures you both survive together against the odds. However, it does not give much room to breathe or grow. This is why Taurus can be accused of stagnation because, in the desire to keep everything the same and to know what belongs to whom, there is no fresh air coming in to breathe new life into a relationship that may have become, dare it be said, a little bit dull.

Many people appreciate being with a rock. Yet after a while, that rock can become a ball and chain. The immoveable object once again that crushes freedom of spirit. Although unwittingly, of course, because Taurus bears no malice and genuinely believes that their relationship style is the right way to go about things. And who is to say otherwise?

So if you are in partnership heaven with a Taurus and have ticked the box marked 'permanent', then know that you are super-glued together. You prefer the 'same old' to the uncertainty of flightier types. You know that Taurus will put up with your foibles, perhaps not without complaint, but they are not going to up and leave just because you squeezed the toothpaste the wrong way. It boils down to trust and in Taurus you have a trustworthy partner. Keep them in affection and culinary delight and you can enjoy a life of ease.

The Ex Factor: Unharnessed, Unyoked

When Taurus makes a commitment, you are both locked in with double padlocks. It takes a Houdini to escape the chains that bind.

Yet when things start to fray around the edges in a relationship with a Taurus, the hard part is that, like the Emperor with his clothes, the bull will swear that there is nothing wrong. As long as you are physically present then you are 'there', or 'theirs'. Taurus may not notice that you have psychologically or emotionally checked out of the relationship because their antennae is not switched on to notice such things. Besides, their expectations for the relationship are relatively simple. You signed up for it (whether in marriage or just by dint of being there for a number of years). Because repetition builds an intense sense of familiarity, safety and security for the bull they may fail to understand how deadening it is for others to be trapped living out Groundhog Day. There is a saying 'familiarity breeds contempt', which is anathema to the bull, who absolutely loves to go to the same restaurant, order the same food and go on the same holiday – and revels in knowing what they are getting. For those of a more adventurous spirit who may have climbed into the safety of the Taurean net, what appeared charmingly reassuring eventually gets just plain boring. The predictability of the marriage bed looks less appealing than the hurly burly of the chaise longue.

The subtleties of deeper emotional exchange may not be registered as missing as long as the everyday factors in life are up and running. This is Taurus's safeguard against injury, yet, of course, it tends to propel them into the very place they are scared of – the deep end. When things go wrong that are not fixable by physical means, Taurus is at a loss and largely unprepared. This sign may be unable to understand what exactly went wrong. If they are the ones who do the leaving, their actions may be just as inexplicable to them. It may simply feel like a physical calling.

Depending on the extenuating circumstances, but particularly if you were with one of those bulls for whom putting food on the table or bringing in the money was their priority, ticking the boxes of 'doing it right', you are likely to experience the full rage of the angry bull. You will be charged at by a ferocious beast, mad at you for not holding it together. For giving that dangerous zone of uncertainty more of your heart than the very thing you had built together over all those years. A bull who has maintained your relationship for years will not take kindly to instant dismissal. It is an affront to their dignity, to their virtues of loyalty, constancy and respect.

It can be a rude awakening for the bull and bring them face-to-face with the very emotional depths they have been trying to avoid all their lives.

The fixity of the bull that was so engaged in preserving the relationship will now be channelled into trying to resuscitate it. If that is impossible then their single-minded, unwavering energy will be expended in making sure that they can hold onto whatever else they have spent energy acquiring and collecting. In other words: do not expect this bull to see reason over anything material you held together. Taurus can be utterly intransigent, so stubborn they will never give up or give in. They will fight for what is theirs – and may see it as all theirs. If, however, it is the bull who chooses to leave a long partnership then they have no doubt planned an exit strategy, even a ceremony where you will be handed over the keys to the car, the window locks, etc., together with instructions on how everything works. Because, of course, you relied on them to do all that kind of thing, didn't you?

Many Taureans find it very hard to let go of their ex, even if they are the ones doing the leaving. It goes back to their innate attitudes towards possession and attachment. For some people, being divorced from a Taurus just means that you have a different financial arrangement but still they see you as belonging to them. They have rights over you. Never forget that this is the most stubborn of signs; relinquishing the past is a total trauma. Having to find their way in a new life, a new reality, is the biggest challenge. However, if they make it, then Taurus can be a solid type of ex, dependably taking care of you in some way. They tend to abide by the rules of the law and because you go back a long way then you will always hold a treasured place of affection in their hearts.

DESTINY

The Taurean Herd Instinct

Taurus flourishes in set-ups and structures where they know the ground rules and what's expected of them. They do like to belong – to a club or organisation – especially those that are tried and tested and have stood the test of time. Although Taurus can hang with the in-crowd, they tend to favour tradition, something a bit more old-fashioned. The history is something that appeals to Taurus and makes it more valuable in their eyes.

As a team player, Taurus is wonderful at managing, organising and ensuring everything works. Aesthetics matter so it will all be done as beautifully as possible and preferably within budget and on time. You see, Taurus has a plan and can strategise for many months or years. They don't need instant results, like some of the other signs, as they are more ponderous and enjoy the build-up as much as the actual accomplishment.

As a friend, Taurus is one of the most stalwart in the zodiac. Doing their utmost to stand by you, loyally there for you and the kind of person who will come over to help you clear out, fix or mend. You can't expect them to be there in a jiffy though – a bit of advance notice is the way they operate. If you've got some kind of crisis they will always work up from the bottom line, steadfastly giving you practical measures to help you resolve whatever is bothering you, even though the whole emotional nuance is not something they choose to address.

Being part of the Taurus team is always going to offer you something of a safety net, a bit of an anchor. Although Taurus themselves will often be attracted to more whimsical types, they will be the person who holds the tribe together. A very important and valuable role.

TAURUS

♉

ALTAR OBJECTS

Place some of these objects on your altar or carry them with you in actual or pictorial form.

*

CRYSTAL: emerald, rose quartz, sapphire

MINERAL/METAL: copper

TAURUS SYMBOLS: the Bull, Venus

TAROT CARD: The Hierophant

ANGEL CARDS: Angel Asmodel, Archangel Chamuel

FLOWERS: rose, foxglove, poppy, sweet william

TREE: maple

SCENTS AND CANDLES: rose, sandalwood, amber

MEMORY BOARD/PHOTOGRAPHS/PICTURES: love letters, people you love; painting: 'Birth of Venus' by Sandro Botticelli

CLOTH: pink or green cashmere or velvet

TALISMAN: Aphrodite, rose quartz jewellery

*

GEMINI

GEMINI

Catch Me If You Can

Ⅱ

CORE QUALITIES: *changeable, pollinator of ideas, restless, people person*

Mantra: Today I will speak from my heart and soul.

Constellation of Gemini: the two bright stars Castor and Pollux each mark a starry eye of a Twin. Best viewed during the winter months, it was described by the 2nd century AD astronomer, Ptolemy.

Gemini is a constantly changing kaleidoscope – as soon as you receive one picture of their personality it instantly morphs into another. They are hard to keep track of, always on the move in their quest to satisfy their curiosity about life. They are the shape-shifters, the distractors and deflectors. It's as if everything is magnetised to them, yet their skin is non-stick and so it all just slips off, leaving Gemini squeaky clean to move on to the next fascination.

Gemini is known to be flirtatious but don't take it too seriously as they are actually flirting with life, trying on so many different scenarios, like outfits, just for fun. Amusement is integral to their enjoyment of life. Geminis are famously light-hearted and part of their magician energy is to make you laugh just when you thought you might cry. They can change the atmosphere in a room so fast just by saying 'Look!' They captivate everyone's attention with their wit and then, like McCavity, disappear into thin air – almost vaporise – so you're left wondering what happened. Don't worry, Gemini just saw something more interesting somewhere else. Don't expect this sign not to look over your shoulder while they are talking to you – their radar scans more busily than air-traffic control. They can also Mercurially mug you of all your contacts, anecdotes and snippets of information, before depositing them elsewhere, repackaged and presented by themselves, as if the messenger is more important than the message.

There is a kind of trickster energy about this sign; they can be like a conjurer, not necessarily of the black arts but nevertheless a little sleight of hand is Gemini's forte. It always leaves you guessing, which is exactly the impression Gemini wishes to create. This sign refuses to be trapped or labelled, which is why they have developed myriad ways to avoid capture.

As Gemini is the sign of the twins, you are always in the presence of duality, whether you know it or not. There will be more than two of you in the relationship because you are with both twins – sometimes simultaneously, other times you get entirely different energy from this person in a split second as the other twin shows up. You can suddenly feel as if you are dealing with a different person! It is pointless to try to make sense of why black is white and white is black when this happens. It just is. It's Gemini's Castor and Pollux calling card and they simply can't help their dual nature. At least it means life is never dull.

Gemini has such a playful attitude towards just about everything in life; they see everything as a game. This absolves them from having to be accountable or to take things seriously. The 'game' mindset comes in handy when it's necessary to recover fast from any misfortunes. Yet, the mental identity of Gemini is so strong that it is hard for them to access their feelings, let alone anyone else's. They are scared of being trapped and unable to move. Gemini suffers from emotional claustrophobia. It is a secret terror of theirs that they will get stuck in the suffocation of an emotional drama. They simply don't want to go there.

Gemini has a knack of deflecting all comments that border emotional territory, making a joke, changing the subject, rationalising everything away. Their approach certainly works to cut off the emotional current and exchange it for talk about almost any other subject!

LIFE

Health

Gemini exudes a nervous energy, as if the wind can change at any moment and they are reading the signals, ready to react in an instant. Their wiring can get so frazzled and fragmented with all the messages they receive from people, their devices and the world spinning around them that their synch mechanisms can unravel from overload.

Mind

As Gemini is picking up information from everyone and everywhere all the time they tend to know a little about everything. The Gemini mind has high-speed processing capabilities that delivers astoundingly bijou pieces of interest culled from thousands of words of back-story. So Gemini will always come up with the salient point, the person you need to talk to, the place you need to visit. They are an absolute treasure trove of information. They love to converse, talking to everyone about anything with their quicksilver mental powers rapidly flitting from subject to subject. Gemini can pull together a mind map of how all interests are connected and how they work together. They have a butterfly mind, alighting on points of interest like bees landing on flowers and achieving fertilisation through carrying information between people and ideas. They are their own giant network and hub, literally buzzing with all you need to know. However, Gemini can suffer from mental exhaustion as they simply don't know how to switch off or stand still. Part of the problem is their need to be constantly well informed, which keeps them glued to news outlets, their iPhone and digital media. Gemini almost feels they will die if they are not updated with what's going on 24/7. It is very hard to separate them from their gadgets – to literally get them to unplug.

Body

The sign of Gemini rules the hands, lungs and nervous system. The saying 'turning their hand to anything' is apt for Gemini who is often a handy type and at the very least possesses a passing acquaintance with anything that requires the capacity to make, sell and do. As the lungs are associated with breathing and air, Geminis benefit greatly from learning how to breathe properly and effectively; literally expelling air from their system enables them to figuratively empty out all the 'stuff' they have taken into themselves. Being highly strung, any means of calming the para-sympathetic nervous system is enormously helpful to this sign. But for Gemini perhaps walking meditation is the best therapy they can do, as they have no wish to be rooted to the spot for too long!

There always remains a youthfulness about Gemini, no matter what age, which radiates a playful quality. They often appear extremely young for their age and this may not have so much to do with their physical looks, but with their minds, which are constantly curious about life, and their agility – both physical and mental – which create a childlike aura about them.

Spirit

The bubbly, bright and breezy Gemini spirit travels light and can be crushed by other people's heavy moods, onerous responsibilities and routine. Gemini needs to come up for air. True to their sylph-like nature, they want to shoot the breeze. The twins can dazzle and delight, yet they need their space, their freedom, to keep ahead of all that's new and developing, rather than getting bogged down in all that is or was. Yesterday's news is never going to interest Gemini.

Of course, they have a tendency to spread themselves too thin, leaving a trail of broken promises, unfinished conversations and even relationships in their wake. Perhaps they figure it's easier to be a moving target in life.

Spiritually and Karmically

Geminis are here to learn and teach, to make connections that help others to understand where and how life fits together. Many Geminis have such a flair for disseminating information that they pursue careers in media, social media and digital platforms – they are the ideas people that create concepts or simply project the gift of the gab that keeps others entertained, informed and amused. London's black-cab driver would be the quintessential Gemini with the constant verbiage and movement, but anyone who moves in the realm of words and ideas is living the Gemini dream. The twins are clever, not necessarily in an intellectual sense but they know how to get their message across. Their special mental gifts are spiritual in the sense that they are not meant exclusively for their own personal use, but to keep the world turning and spinning on its axis.

What Does Gemini Have to Give?

Gemini's multi-dimensional angles on life provide so much liveliness and interest. They are the spin doctors who can quickly change tack and emphasis. Geminis have an immediate sense of what others need to know, the gap in the market, the USP of the brand and where it belongs in the wider world. For those who simply don't have the time, inclination or curiosity to find out such things, talking to a Gemini provides instant updates on the world around them. Hermes, the messenger and symbol of the Gemini planet Mercury, is essentially a guide. He can take you places, lead you to the right answer. With Gemini you never need satnav ever again!

If you enjoy lively, sparky conversation then you will be enthralled by the Gemini take on just about everything. However, this sign is often accused of being a Jack of All Trades and Master of None – and for those looking for substance, Gemini's superficiality and glibness can be found lacking. Socially skilled to the nth degree, you will never find Gemini at a loss for words as they can find the common denominator that puts people together. In fact, getting a kick out of making introductions, networking and facilitating the opening of doors for others is what brings Gemini alive. The twins do not jealously guard their ideas or their contacts and are outstandingly generous in terms of putting people in touch with each other. It is always a case of the more the merrier with Gemini, who has never grasped the concept of personal space for the two of you!

Their sheer animation is a wonder to behold and rubs off on others, often sparking interests in people that amount to a new lease of life. Talking to Gemini is like taking word medicine!

What Does Gemini Need to Receive?
Gemini is an Air sign and therefore they need to be brought down to earth in order to manifest their ideas. This is why Gemini is

often attracted to earthy types (Taurus, Virgo or Capricorn) who anchor them in reality. Instead of always moving on to the next thing, Gemini can be helped to focus on the one brilliant idea and to make it real by manifesting something concrete from it. Gemini can also benefit from investigating deeper into a relationship or subject, instead of being all skittish and taking off just when the subject requires practical action.

On the subject of feelings, the evolutionary path of Gemini is to dare to enter the field of the heart, to respond with compassion rather than analysis. To give value to people's feelings rather than crush them with reason. Asking Gemini what they feel and accompanying them into the emotional realm can be a huge catalyst for this sign to recognise how important their feelings are.

What Does Gemini Need to Learn?

Gemini never has a problem with learning, although concentration can be an issue. No, their minds are more open than a sieve, yet somehow they feel perpetually dissatisfied with what they already know because something much more interesting must be around the corner. To a certain extent, all Geminis lead double lives. Their twin energies simply cannot be united and there is the tendency towards splitting. This means they are often in two minds, or their head says one thing and their heart another. Perhaps they split their time between two cities, places, careers or loves. Or they really are into that double energy and live half a life here on planet Earth, with their astral body flying into another dimension, living their 'unlived' life. That Peter Pan energy is very prevalent in Geminis – the desire not to get tied down or grow up. The problem with Gemini can be fragmentation, too many pieces, leading to loss of soul energy. Gemini has to cultivate a strong sense of self, like a spine that holds everything together.

Instead of jumping around, Gemini could become inquisitive about the qualities of consistency and reliability. The saying 'talk is cheap' reflects on Gemini's verbal skills, which may sound good but lack the real substance that is knowledge. Developing the mature approach of knowing when to hold on is essential to Gemini's growth.

LOVE

Dating: Double Dating the Twins

The effervescence of Gemini is so seductive, their charm and repartee so engaging, you would have to have a heart of stone to spurn them when they first set their sights on you. For a start they can instantly pick up a point of reference that connects you and before you know it you are chatting away like old friends. Moving swiftly from subject to subject, Gemini is all the while scanning you and mentally processing what you are all about. You will feel as if you are the most interesting person in the room. Unless, of course, you are not! In which case, Gemini will speedily move on – and with the flimsiest of excuses that leaves you wondering if you should change your deodorant!

For the most part, dating a Gemini is like witnessing a variety show. You never know what is going to happen next. Each date is totally different from the last and each contains a myriad of experiences and people. Yes, there will be other people. If you like intimate soirees, just the two of you, then you may be sorely disappointed when Gemini arrives with their friends in tow or explains casually just as you are sitting down to dinner, that some interesting people are in town they would like you to meet. Failing that, Gemini will simply start a conversation with the people at the next table. You are left with the impression that you are not enough to hold their attention. Rule Number One: You can't, so don't expect to. Gemini has to constantly check their phone, rush out to get something or say hello to someone – it's part of their nature. Rule Number Two: Don't take it personally. The constant need for distraction does not mean you are dull and boring. It is just in the DNA of Gemini to move about, fiddle with things, add people into the mix – you get the picture. Besides they have such an all-consuming mental curiosity that unless you are dating them in the desert there is bound to be something to distract them. Although, even in the desert Gemini would no doubt find a lone cactus or sand dune that attracts their attention.

To spark the interest of Gemini and keep them coming back for more you have to be intriguing. Not in a heavy way because Gemini runs a mile from anything they perceive as threateningly deep – especially on a date, which must be kept amusing, light and full of fabulous fun. The butterfly nature of Gemini – a beautiful, ethereal, air-bound creature – means you can't think of 'catching' them, merely attracting their interest.

Ask questions, remain slightly tantalising yourself and Gemini will feed off your nectar. Pretty soon you will have them in the palm of your hand. But keep it open.

If you want to date a Gemini, the good news is that you can take them absolutely anywhere, even several places in a single evening, without fazing them one bit. Don't worry about moving between A and B – Gemini loves to walk, hop on a rickshaw, hail an uber, take the river bus or hire a bike. They are literally poetry in motion and the more movement the better.

The experience is what it's all about for Gemini so they are just as happy grazing on street food as going to some swanky eatery. You want to leave them buzzing, not longing to escape.

If you make it past the first date and are seeing Gemini more often then it pays to be mindful that any form of being tied down can trouble this sign. They will do anything to avert a potential attack of emotional claustrophobia!

The Gemini is fifty shades of everything, so you never know what you're going to get. Besides, the issue of the twins – and undoubtedly you can date one of them and be sacked by the other – means there is that constant changeability inherent in their nature and they can alter direction like the wind. This is especially evident in their communication. Plans can chop and change rapidly and Gemini will never understand that this can be irritating for the other person, since they themselves thrive on adapting to changing situations.

Gemini can, however, string you along when you are going out with them. You might get the feeling that you are one of many. It's not beyond feasibility that this is the case if you are dealing with multi-tasking Gemini! Dating a Gemini is a lesson in non-attachment. The less you cling, the more their own tendrils will wrap around you.

It's essential, however, that you maintain your own life, friends and interests rather than attempting full immersion in your relationship with Gemini. They will appreciate you more for being your own person and bringing new experiences to them. You may do best keeping things short and sweet with them until they are ready to move to the next level. The key with Gemini is to make the sharing of experiences very enjoyable, so that you can talk about them together during and afterwards and to keep new people and elements coming in. This is the way to their heart so that you become that essential person with whom they want to share the excitement of life.

When you date a Gemini you are essentially brain fodder and as such must be able to give them food for thought. If you can zip around several subjects simultaneously, so much the better because Gemini will love to join the dots in your thinking. If you can deal with the constant interruptions to your togetherness, handle the juggling act that Gemini performs and even pick up the occasional ball they have dropped, you will gain free entry into the Gemini world and access to 'the messenger of the gods', which is Gemini in their finest form as Hermes – the only god who could get in anywhere!

Keeping . . . the Conversation Going
If things get serious with a Gemini – and it's hard to tell as they don't really do commitment per se in a loved-up other-half kind of way – they could find you indispensable as their muse, their sounding board, even their anchor (which Gemini needs, even though they can slip it from time to time). However, you will detect an almost imperceptible shift which amounts to them keeping you constantly in the loop, asking your opinion instead of telling you theirs. The way to tame a twin is through the mind and you must develop skills similar to a horse whisperer, giving freedom and developing trust that keeps Gemini coming back to you.

Recognise too that even if you have managed to get Gemini to the altar you still only have a piece of them, but if it's their heart then it's for real. Gemini can't bear to be suffocated by too much intimacy; they need constant room to breathe, to do their own thing, meet people and keep life interesting. They will never lose their playful energy as long as you don't impose heavy regulations. It is always best to allow a Gemini to come to you rather than try to cling to them, otherwise they will brush you off unless it is their own choice to have you there.

As a long-term partner, Gemini will maintain the freshness of the relationship as if you have just met. This will be a meeting of minds, shared interests and activities that will never descend into a rut. However, domestic duties must be interspersed with more stimulating activities. Don't expect Gemini to keep the home fires burning without plenty of outside entertainment.

There are bound to be many comings and goings on the home front, perhaps a never-ending stream of visitors and a packed schedule that leaves hardly any downtime. Gemini believes that they should be living life to the full, making the most of every minute. Which is why the routine tasks are often delegated to people who enjoy changing light bulbs whilst Gemini prefers the mental light-bulb moment!

If you are an earthy Taurus, Virgo or Capricorn or a watery Cancer, Scorpio or Pisces then you could find yourself picking up after Gemini, becoming the chief cook and bottle washer. Unless you have got a twin with significant nesting instincts in their chart or one who has evolved beyond the *puer* (eternal youth) mentality, you have your work cut out on the home front.

Much is made of Gemini's tricksy nature so it would be easy to assume that they have a string of lovers. But this is not usually the case! Your Gemini is perhaps more likely to be mentally unfaithful in terms of chatting to others. The boundaries have to be laid down in advance so Gemini knows where the line is, but equally keeping your own conversation with Gemini going is essential.

Nothing turns them off faster than tears, emotional dramas and heavy subjects. They drown under the oppression of accusations and expectations. You might have been married to them for ten years but when you take offence that Gemini has forgotten your wedding anniversary you will get that blank look. What do you mean they don't care? They are with you, aren't they? Gemini can make it up with spontaneous gestures that melt you with their childlike delight. If you are the type who needs constant reassurance of their devoted love for you, then this won't be a match made in heaven. Gemini will need to constantly scratch that mental itch. But if you keep the door open and that mental spark between you remains, they will always walk back through.

The Ex Factor

Once Gemini's mind has gone elsewhere for a period of time and it has become impossible to reel them back in, then you have to accept they have mentally left – even if you are still washing their socks.

The most common factor in the Gemini break-up is feeling trapped by boredom, responsibility and routine. Of course, in mature adult life, learning to deal with these things is a rite of passage. Geminis who can cross this threshold make amazing partners. Otherwise, this sign can look pretty sad as an eternal Peter Pan who just can't settle down for long. Of course, they will never admit the great loss of intimacy and togetherness because they will fly into their new future so fast, perhaps even making up for lost time with a dizzying array of delights that convinces them this is the life well lived. However, that duality of Gemini is still there and underneath their bright and busy life might lie a certain emotional emptiness.

As Gemini doesn't want to be dragged into an emotional mire, any divorce or separation is often dealt with from Gemini's point of view on a logical basis. But, of course, any heart-felt union is bound to end with sadness. Recriminations are pointless and really you need to keep those lines of communication open. When all the nasty legal bits are done, what you may have left is still a great mental connection that transcends all past hurt. It is perfectly possible to have a 'good' relationship with your Gemini ex – perhaps even a better one than you had whilst you were married – once the chains are broken and Gemini sees themselves as free.

If you ditch a Gemini after a long-term partnership it is possible they will pull the other twin on you and you'll suddenly see another side of them. They could want you back if they can't have you and many couples get caught in the push-me-pull-you of the twin energy that is essentially too fractured to be glued back together again.

Emotionally, it can be hard to deal with the master-of-deflection kind of Gemini who will accept no portion of blame or responsibility for what happened between you. Unless you have things in writing, Gemini is also capable of claiming that the exact opposite of your own truth took place.

In terms of fighting over material assets, of course Gemini is a born negotiator and can strip an asset quicker than you can call your accountant. However, their dual nature works brilliantly in terms of division of what you have. Gemini really gets the idea of splitting things in two, although they can't help whisking away what you thought was solid! Gemini can distract you by spinning information in all directions so that you take your eye off the ball just at a crucial moment. Their Mercurial nature is adept at swiftly turning the tables, giving out misinformation and performing card tricks that keep both you and your lawyer guessing as to what is really going on.

As a parent, Gemini can thrive in a joint custody scenario – it is absolutely right up their street, giving them the chance to be free exactly half the time and then being a family person for the other half. There are many Gemini parents who say they have a better relationship with their children now that they have this arrangement. They also enjoy making their time with the children educational, fun and busy. Perhaps now that your extra child, the kid-adult that is Gemini, has left your home, you can better appreciate what they have to offer.

DESTINY

The Gemini Jamboree – Join In

Gemini was made for networking. They absolutely love to introduce people, connect them, build groups that link people of like minds. Gemini is indeed a one-person think-tank and when they put their minds to stimulating others, they can initiate amazing events, activities and get-togethers.

They handle people so deftly that everyone wants to be part of what Gemini is orchestrating. The one prerequisite if you want to be on Gemini's team is to be 'interesting'. This quality is of the greatest value to the twins, nothing less will do.

Besides, this sign is really its own media outlet – disseminating ideas, interviewing people constantly (yes, if you have a Gemini friend you will always be asked what you think about everything) and collecting information that is useful to everyone and, above all, highly engaging.

Socially skilled to the nth degree, this sign has a gift for bringing people together and making them all feel it is better to be part of something than to go it alone.

GEMINI

Ⅱ

ALTAR OBJECTS

Place some of these objects on your altar or carry them with you in actual or pictorial form.

*

CRYSTAL: quartz, sodalite

MINERAL/METAL: quicksilver

GEMINI SYMBOLS: Hermes, messenger of the gods, twins

TAROT CARDS: The Lovers, The Magician

ANGEL CARDS: Angel Ambriel, Archangel Zadkiel

FLOWERS: lily of the valley

TREE: ash

SCENTS AND CANDLES: lavender, mint family: spearmint, peppermint

MEMORY BOARD/PHOTOGRAPHS/PICTURES: inspirational quotes, social activities, memberships; painting: 'Mercury and Paris' by Donato Creti

CLOTH: mesh or net gauze – pale yellow

TALISMAN: Hermes, butterfly

*

CANCER

CANCER

Comfort Zone

CORE QUALITIES: *caring, instinctual, empathic, searching for security*

Mantra: I will not take anything personally, even if it is meant personally.

The constellation of Cancer: Cancer is one of the faintest constellations in the sky, yet is visible in both the Northern and Southern hemispheres.

The Moon-ruled crab is an ambivalent creature who lives half by land and half by sea. This mirrors the extrovert/introvert part of the Cancerian psychological make-up, fluctuating between yang – outgoing and expressive – and yin – clam-shut with a shell so defensively barricaded that the crab's retreat into its interior world means no one will be allowed inside. In the ancient Song dynasty period (AD 960–1279) the Chinese symbol for yin and yang was associated with the light and dark phases of the Moon. Of course, as the Moon itself is in a state of perpetual motion with the quickest orbit of any of the heavenly bodies – showing us nothing as a New Moon, then a delicate crescent, then half, then waxing into its fullness – it's hardly surprising that Cancerians can seem mesmerising. It's as if you can't quite get hold of them because of their capacity to shut down and then reveal. You never quite know what you're going to get. However, you can be sure that whatever it is will change again like the tides.

Yet however unfathomable you may find Cancer, you can be sure that they have already picked up on who you are and what you're all about. Cancer is one of the most intuitive signs of the zodiac and their instincts are usually spot on. You won't necessarily have told them a thing, but they have sensed what is going on and importantly what you might need. Cancer has a nose for such things. There is no point trying to fool them because they have read all your non-verbal clues, your energy field and the vibrations you hold around you. There is no place to hide.

As Cancerians need to be needed and are almost pathologically empathic, they may offer you just what your soul is yearning for. They understand where you're coming from and can soothe your spirit with their uniquely comforting words, understanding glances and personable energy. Perhaps your paths crossed because of a business meeting, but Cancer will make a personal connection with you that is unforgettable. Of course, if you are one of those linear types that wants to brush off awkward feelings and keep your facades intact, then you might find Cancer slightly invasive. It's not that they push – but you can't help knowing that they KNOW! Some signs are spooked by the intensely personal nature of their gaze but they won't use this power as one-upmanship over you. In fact, they genuinely wish to help and, being sensitive to rejection, any perceived slight will send them scuttling back into their shell.

LIFE

Health

As a Water sign, Cancer soaks up what's around them and whatever is taken in can affect their wellbeing for good or ill. Bad
vibes can literally cause stomach upsets; unspoken anger can trigger
a headache. Yet, they do possess their own perfectly formed defence
system in the form of their shell. This, however, can be left open
or remain closed at the wrong moments! Cancer is associated with
the breasts – they nurture others, taking them into their care;
and also the stomach – they have a gut instinct for what's wrong.

Mind

The Cancerian mind is like a sponge. They learn through osmosis
rather than factual observation and therefore they soak up what is
around them, both literally and spiritually. They are open to all that
is subliminal and the imaginative and poetic realm. Being a hugely
subjective sign it can be very hard for the crab to stand outside of
their own perceptions to get any level of detachment and objectivity.
This can make them infuriating, but the most extraordinary thing
is that they are usually right! As in Malcom's Gladwell's *Blink*, they
have a perception that takes in what is not obvious to others. They
are a genius at reading the subtle realms that others miss and therefore their pincers are right on the button. As such, the crab is in a
provocative place where the actual real world perhaps doesn't mean
as much to them as their impression of it. Evidential, material reality
collides with the reality of the intangible senses.

Cancerians are marvellous raconteurs as they have such an
enchanting ability to relive personal anecdotes and have hugely
impressive memories that won't forget the colour, detail and
nuance that brings every story to life. In fact, crabs do not live

in linear time but a world where the past is concurrent with the present. What happened a few years ago is as vivid to them as what is happening right now. They have a particular knack of collapsing the space-time continuum and a craving to explore history and make nostalgic trips down memory lane.

Body

There is something peculiarly liquid about Cancer. Whether it is the beautiful, limpid, shining eyes or the round, Moon-faced appearance, just looking at them, you feel drawn into their tenderness. Their skin is soft to the touch, unless of course they have developed a hard crustacean shell together with the bony New Moon nose or rounder Moon face.

As a Water sign, crabs are primarily receptive, taking in all that surrounds them and as such they can become overloaded. This can back up in the system as fluid retention – as if all emotional nuances have been retained in the body. Cancer is the sign of the Great Mother and is associated with breasts and breastfeeding as primordial nurturing. In ancient mythology, the Milky Way itself was thought of as the breast milk of the Great Mother spread across the constellations, nurturing the cosmos. The stomach is also connected with the sign of Cancer – the place where nourishing food is broken down – as well as the gut (something Cancer has in common with Virgo) and for the crab, in particular, gut instincts.

Spirit

In terms of energy, the crab can vacillate between highly active energy and feeling wiped out. Much of this is to do with what has been picked up in the outside atmosphere rather than being dictated by their own energy sources. Cancer needs to learn how to protect itself from being drained by other people.

The crab needs spiritual sustenance – for their soul to be nourished as much as they nourish others. Otherwise they can become fodder for those in need, who take so much out of them that their life force and emotional energy become severely depleted.

Spiritually and Karmically
Cancerians hold an emotional attunement that centres around bonding, nurturing and attaching to those close to them. The vibration of Cancer is essentially emotional, their spirits both uplifted and impacted by the energies they receive all around them. Cancer incarnates with strong needs for personal attachment and a sense of having significant karma with family members. Working through family dynamics, particularly about their mother, is a major part of their soul journey. Frequently, the Cancer clan is highly enmeshed, or there is a lot of unconscious emotion that keeps the crab trapped in issues from the past and working through a series of emotional obligations. There can be a lot of ghosts to lay to rest and many Cancerians are psychically connected to their ancestors or to homes or land that have been in the family for generations. They do experience huge connections to particular places and the sense of feeling 'at home' in certain locations or buildings is of paramount importance to them. It is not unknown for Cancer to get a sense of déjà vu when they walk in somewhere for the first time and feel they have been there before. A flashback from a past life perhaps.

The Cancerian karma is therefore centred around creating a

safe place, sometimes translated as an actual home, but symbolically meaning inner security. Blood ties are paramount, yet Cancer also has a way of collecting non-blood members of a tribe, a clan that 'feels like family'. When meeting people, Cancer can easily detect just by looking at and reading that person whether 'they are one of us'. Inevitably this can create trouble, an us-versus-them situation, with the crab battening down the hatches against perceived intruders.

What Does Cancer Have to Give?
No matter what sex the crab happens to be, they channel the Divine Mother energy. They are heavily invested in looking after people, helping them develop and taking care of them – whether they are friend, family or business associate. Cancer can extend their pincers to helping anyone in need. The stranger in the street, the person lost and looking – if Cancer's antenna has picked up on you, then they are there for you.

Cancer's gift for creating homes spills out to anyone who spends time in their abode. Whether it's just a couple of rooms or a vast mansion, Cancer will somehow imbue the atmosphere with that sense that hits you as soon as you visit: you have come home. There is no point trying to sell a house to Cancer if they can't detect a whiff of 'home'. They can turn a tent into an entrancing personal space you will never want to leave, but if the vibe doesn't sit well with the crab, something in the air doesn't feel right, they will never be able to make it their own.

Cancer will look after you, sometimes making you feel childlike in the face of their parental parading. However, they mean so well, have a genuine desire to protect and guide you, so you just have to take that slice of homemade cake home with you. Their true forte is in their astounding capacity to pick up exactly what is wrong with you in the first place. There is no hiding from the crab, who is extremely sensitive towards hurts and wounds that exist in others behind the smiley face. Once you receive those silvery rays of their Moon-vibe into your being, you realise that being connected to a crab is a blessing.

What Does Cancer Need to Receive?
As a Water sign, Cancer can flounder in the tides, drowning in sensitivity and very much in need of an anchor. It takes a brave soul to point out gently to Cancer that it might be best not to take everything personally. However, this is exactly what they need to understand. If you hand them the lifeline of detachment, they may balk at it, wondering how on earth it is relevant to their FEELINGS! But in the long run they will thank you for it, as they find their way back to centre with the help of a little room to breathe between their own perception and someone else's.

Equally it can be helpful for Cancer to recognise that people have their own lives and are perfectly capable of tying their own shoelaces! Even if Cancer is affronted at first, they will respect you more if the balance of power is more evenly distributed between you, with the knob turned down on their care and control.

What Does Cancer Need to Learn?
If Cancer can recognise that their own moods, like the tides and phases of the Moon itself, are subject to daily fluctuations then they can begin to gain some distance, to get in touch with their own essence beyond the emotional flux. In other words, they are

more than just their feelings, which can become, like the monkey mind, rather wearing. Finding stillness, peace and calm is their lesson. In this they can practice not responding, reacting and reaching out. Eventually Cancer has to learn that just being, or even being there, is enough. This way they develop a barrier between their core self and the energies that are constantly circulating in the atmosphere and will find that they feel stronger, happier and have more life essence available to them as it is not being sapped by the feeling states of either themselves or other people.

As a rule, the crab does best when it learns how to cut those ties that bind. Far from casting them adrift, being free of other people's demands is immensely liberating for them. Of course, as the nature of Cancer is to attach themselves, they will always seek emotional connection, but ensuring the hangers on are disconnected (psychically, through the creative visualisation of unhooking them from their energy field perhaps) as well as through developing stronger boundaries, is enormously freeing.

LOVE

Dating: Full Moon Fever

The dating pool can be where Cancer feels lost. A crab lost at sea. Adrift in the oceanic depths of people, possibilities, feelings and fantasies. With so much flotsam and jetsam out there on the net, the crab often retreats into its shell, for fear of being made prey. As Cancer picks up all that is circulating in the atmosphere, the entire social media dating network can feel overwhelming. For Cancer, familiarity is key. They prefer old-school dating. Not that Aunt Maude has to formally introduce the nice boy or girl from across the road, but there has to be some kind of connection that harks back to familiar ground, landmarks, people, experiences or places in common. This gives the crab something tangible to hold on to. A new experience can be built on an existing one, which creates safety for this very sensitive sign.

So if you want to make it past swiping right, then it's best to put out some personal 'hooks' that will get the crab's pincers attached. Some old photos, favourite places – being yourself is essential. However, if you chance upon a crab in 'real' life then you are given a much better opportunity to engage. Cancerians like to discuss what things mean to them so the personal question is not one to be avoided when first meeting. If you think date conversation with a crab should cover jobs, CVs, earning capacity and net worth, please understand that this will leave the crab totally cold. The sooner those personal chords are connected between you, the easier it will be to build bridges that lead to an emotionally fulfilling relationship. Were you thinking of something else?! Let's get this straight, emotional fulfilment is numero uno for Cancer – nothing else really matters. So a flash in the pan isn't their style.

For Cancer to consider dating you, there has to be an unmistakeable connection between you. Cancer likes to be comfortable and relaxed. To feel 'at home' with you. If they are not at ease, this thing will never fly. Another curious thing about Cancer is that like their symbol of the crab they tend to move sideways rather than making a direct approach. They can literally sidle up to you, sit down next to you and strike up a conversation. They dislike being too obvious, so you can expect them to make their move rather indirectly. This is also because of their inherent fear of rejection.

Cancer is usually fluid and flexible with arrangements, as long as dates are not in 'scary' places – too many people, too much going on. The crab wants to be able to focus on the two of you, to actually listen to what you're saying, so gentle mood lighting and an atmosphere of intimacy is best. If the crab is taking you out, then it will most probably be to one of their favourite haunts. That is unless you have been invited 'home' (an invitation to their nest is a sure sign they really like you). If, however, you're being taken to one of their special places, the amount of back-slapping, hugging and camaraderie you'll see on arrival is to let you know that you are being introduced to 'the tribe'. Cancer usually goes back years with these tribe members, because shared history is enormously bonding for them. Nothing better than a walk through the nostalgic memories that have glued them together. Even if they have never met outside the restaurant, the crab thinks of these people as a touchstone and reference point. You will get the once-over and even the distinct feeling that these people know Cancer so well that your date is either rubber stamped or deemed a disaster from the start.

Very quickly, if you have passed this initial test, you will be introduced to a family member or perhaps be handed the phone to make their acquaintance. Never forget for one second that clan members, whether they are blood or blood-brothers, form a tightly knit unit around the crab. Cancer is inseparable from the people they are close to, so if you want to date a crab then you must fit in, connect and bond with the other members. This doesn't mean you won't get a lot of 'alone time', because Cancer guards their privacy and will ensure they can have you all to themselves without prying eyes. However, the wider Cancer clan is always there, perhaps invisibly so. You can get the distinct feeling that they are listening in somehow – rather unnerving for some signs, especially those who value being free and independent of intrusion, such as Aries and Aquarius.

In the bedroom, Cancer is a tender and affectionate lover. But the surroundings have to be right. They have that Goldilocks tendency towards vetoing whatever is just too little or too much of . . . Don't expect your crab to feel passion unless you've created some kind of a nest for them to sink into. It could be a hammock or a four poster bed, but make sure it is soft, comfortable and, above all, romantic.

Dating a crab who is born under the silvery rays of the Moon can be an emotional minefield, simply because their moods can change so quickly. Was it something you said? Did the wind change direction, did the Moon change its phase? Often, the reason for the change in temperature is imperceptible, but the crab has shifted their inner state from warm, affable and open to chilly, cold and crabby. You are expected to know why this happened (if it is indeed something you said or did in Cancer's eyes) or at the

very least to pick up on it and accept that you've entered a different zone. It can be confusing for those who aren't used to reading
the more obvious clues, or who lack the insight or emotional
intelligence to recognise what has injured the crab. Once Cancer
has slipped inside their shell, it can be a hard job to coax them
out again.

You might be getting the impression that dating a Cancerian
is a tricky business. But that would be doing this delightful sign
a disservice. Who else can convince you after just one meeting
that you have known them forever? Who else but Cancer can
create such a wonderful space between you and hold it open so
that you always feel like an honoured guest, even if you've been
dating for years. Who but Cancer would remember your mother's
birthday, the exact look on your face when you first said 'I love
you' (and most probably even the phase of the Moon, especially
if it was full).

Which brings us on to full Moons and their effect on this
Moonchild. Whilst many people find it harder to sleep under the
Full Moonbeams, Cancer is like a Jellicle cat, recharging their
batteries. Full Moon fever is a natural monthly occurrence for
those born under this lunar-ruled sign. Their hormone levels rise,
their feelings surface, their imagination surges, they suddenly open
up or close down. So don't expect your Cancerian to be demure
or rational at Full Moon. They are most likely to be found dancing
in the kitchen, waving their pincers around, staring dreamily out
of the window or gazing in reverie at their beloved silver orb.
Their talisman in all its majesty and mystery.

Keeping . . . the Home Fires Burning

If you're living with or marrying a Cancerian then you are a lucky person, especially if you too revere the whole idea of home and the family unit. For a start, the chances are that you have bagged yourself a domestic god or goddess. Nothing to be sniffed at in these crash-pad times. Cancer invented the acronym TLC and you will receive it. Daily. Perhaps even hourly at first! Their specific kind of doting energy works wonders on those frazzled souls who never find the time to care for themselves. However, some signs find the whole concept of being 'looked after' rather infantilising and baulk at having to surrender their independence to the nanny state! With a little tactful training, Cancer can learn to back off enough for you to tie your own shoelaces, which restores the adult-to-adult balance. However, nurturing you is their default setting and impossible to eradicate (should you even think of such a thing).

House and home is the natural setting in which Cancer shines. This sign exudes either a huge matriarchal or paterfamilias energy. If you share their domain then inevitably you will be living in a proper home whether it's a bedsit or a mega-mansion. No other sign can create that feeling of home like Cancer. Their style is personal, comfortable, a little whimsical (being packed with nostalgia and memorabilia, not to mention heirlooms, keepsakes and quaint bits and pieces picked up here and there). Special plates and dishes exist for every purpose and occasion, bedrooms are heavenly havens and the entire place is one big sanctuary to protect against the outside world. Perhaps Cancer is trying to recreate the comfort of the womb to compensate for the shock of having been born. However, the partner of a Cancer has to learn to live with what they might deem 'clutter', which to Cancer is an intensely personal attachment to an object or belonging.

Talking about attachment, again no other sign attaches quite like Cancer. Once those pincers are in you, then they tenaciously hold on, come what may. The security of maintaining attachments is of paramount importance to Cancer. They are not about to let you go from their pincer grip. This clinging disguises their vulnerability; they are that mushy creature that is super sensitive and fears exposure. It's a bit like the Eagles' classic song 'Hotel California': 'You can check out but you can never leave!

For many signs, a Cancer union is felt to be true domestic bliss. Never mind the occasional sulk, resentment and constant motion between super-soft and tough love, even the emotional fluxes are felt to be TLC of a kind. Cancer channels Divine Mother energy whether they are a parent or not. Being with them makes you feel as if you have come home and as they are a family person it is a rare crab who won't accept your own kith and kin. Cancer is all about sustaining life. Even if you have a hermit crab, they will support partners and children.

The Ex Factor: Curtain Call with an Encore

If things go wrong between you and your crab then you will experience the maelstrom of human emotion that rages and rolls as a thunderstorm. If even this can't clear the air between you, expect many tears (rain showers) and recriminations. For Cancer, who is tightly bound to you, it is almost impossible to let go. Their fear of abandonment can run so deep that if 'the end' has actually happened, the crab is bound to feel devastated. Their wounds and cuts can heal but leave scars that they revisit even years afterwards. The long-lost love, the one that got away, the partner who cut loose – this is a tragedy for Cancer who thrives on continuity, safety and security and enjoys long forays into the emotional journeys of the past. For years afterwards, Cancer holds this relationship in their pincers. Some try to revive it, give it another try, when all others would have lost hope long ago.

As Cancer has no doubt devoted so much of their time and care to a partnership, if it breaks down there can be much resentment. Only in this instance does Cancer recognise that perhaps they have given too much to the other person and have been taken for granted. The partner may actually have felt suffocated.

If Cancer is the one who ups and leaves, it is because there has been a complete lack of emotional understanding on the part of the partner. They will have stayed put for a while and finally retreated into their shell to nurse their wounds, before feeling so rejected that there is no way back. Some Cancerians look to be rescued from these kinds of situations and their capacity to build emotional bonds means that they are susceptible to more emotionally intelligent partners who offer them what is lacking at home. If Cancer does not receive understanding or their sensitive feelings are permanently on edge around a partner who has no time for their mood swings, then even the strongest karmic chords can fray, loosen and break.

Undoubtedly, as an ex, Cancer can sometimes use manipulation, playing on the past, the children, even the weak spots of both themselves and their erstwhile partner in order to hook back into their partner's feelings. Most often said about a Cancerian ex where there are children involved is that they were and are an absolutely great mum or dad. Even when the love between two partners has died, there is no taking away that Cancer's gift for parenthood is superlative.

Where the crab is unable to move on emotionally or let go of an ex, they can cling tenaciously to the family home. It is Cancer who will cry over every last bit of family treasure that is lost to separation or divorce. Sometimes, though, emotional connections and bonds are maintained so well – Cancer thinks nothing of inviting the ex back into their home for family celebrations – that the veil between two worlds is thin and it can feel almost as if nothing has changed, even the skirmishes!

The guilt Cancer feels about breaking up a home can remain an everlasting trigger. This is why the crab needs to do some serious chord-cutting with exes in order to liberate themselves from the memories, attachments and emotional chains that bind.

DESTINY

The Tribe: Clan Cancer

Those born under the sign of Cancer have a natural ability to invisibly signal to you that you are part of their special clan. You feel 'like family' and will be treated as such (with all its ups and downs!). Cancer is an expert at recognising who belongs to them, who will share the same air, who holds the same emotional theme tunes. You may look like chalk and cheese, but that has nothing to do with it. For Cancer, the clan is connected by virtue of the emotional energy field, nothing more tangible than that.

Their friends can go back a long way, but there is always room for a new person who fits. Shared memories and nostalgia knit the whole thing together and the Cancer clan is exceptionally close, hanging out together, supporting each other, there for each other through thick and thin.

If Cancer is part of a work team, they look after each member and form personal connections. They are not good with being moved about too often, having people thrust upon them or being made to adapt to new circumstances. Their speciality is in creating a sense of belonging that unites people beyond the task at hand. Cancer appeals to hearts and like minds – it is never just a case of whoever happens to be around.

CANCER

ALTAR OBJECTS

Place some of these objects on your altar or carry them with you in actual or pictorial form.

*

CRYSTAL: moonstone, rhodonite

MINERAL/METAL: silver

CANCER SYMBOLS: the crab, the Moon

TAROT CARD: The Chariot

ANGEL CARDS: Angel Muriel, Archangel Gabriel

FLOWERS: white flowers

TREE: fir

SCENTS AND CANDLES: jasmine, blackcurrant, lotus

MEMORY BOARD/PHOTOGRAPHS/PICTURES: the family, the beach, childhood, home; painting: 'The Starry Night' by Vincent Van Gogh

CLOTH: fine white, pale grey cotton with silver decoration

TALISMAN: moon symbol jewellery

*

LEO

LEO

Sun King

♌

CORE QUALITIES: *radiant, positive, big heart, charismatic, entitled*

Mantra: Today I will shine brightly on unexpected faces and places, creating light in the shadows.

The constellation of Leo: Leo is in the Northern Celestial hemisphere underneath The Plough. There are seventy stars in the constellation of Leo visible to the naked eye, with the principle star being Cor Leonis (Lion's Heart).

Leo is a BIG person – not necessarily large in frame, but they are always impressive, noticeable and radiate warmth. When you stand next to the Sun King or Queen it is like being bathed in sunshine. That is, unless you have found a particularly needy ego which can relegate you to standing in their shadow, shivering, whilst they soak up every speck of attention and light in the atmosphere. Usually though, Leo is a generous spirit, freely emitting their own solar fire which is so palpable that you naturally gravitate towards it.

Leo is nearly always surrounded by an entourage. Such a majestic presence requires an army of helpers and hangers-on in order to keep the show on the road. The lion king does well in a leadership role, directing the proceedings with plenty of minions to execute their wishes. Because, of course, no one can do it as well as Leo, no one else possesses the creativity, flair and brilliance to make things special. This is the Leo birthright. Challenge it if you will, but people have been sent to the the Tower for less. Insurrection by subordinates is often punished by excommunication. When you are around Leo, you must defer to them, honour them and keep them on that pedestal or throne. A deposed lion is a sad sight, although often a great lesson in humility is learned which ultimately makes Leo a better ruler next time around – because the lion will never remain just a civilian for long.

The glamazon Leo will dazzle you with their golden presence, tossing their lion's mane and giving the impression that their life is wall-to-wall luxury, even if they haven't quite made it yet. If you follow a Leo, you will either be at the best or the most up-and-coming address, since Leo doesn't do down and out. They literally must be seen in all the best places. They always present well because appearances are important to them. Arbiters of style, they favour the best quality, creating a look that showcases their innate pizzazz. Dressing up is also a nod to their performing skills – as Leo is always an actor, whether they are on stage or walking down the high street. Their persona is carefully crafted and their penchant for playing to the gallery means they tend to draw a crowd, or at the very least, plenty of attention.

Of course, Leo can be bossy and dominating. Yet they inspire love very easily as they are quite simply adorable. If you love to love then you will get on with Leo very well, as no one loves life quite like Leo and it's infectious! Leos will always try to create the best time possible. They can conjure up entertainment, fun and fabulous occasions that make memories. They are born to put on a show and all you have to do is turn up. And, of course, admire what they have done – but why wouldn't you?

LIFE

Health

Leo is synonymous with the heart chakra – their capacity to give out love can be experienced as a great healing force for others. Their presence can be life-enhancing and a great tonic for those more repressed types. Yet Leo needs to be able to truly and creatively express themselves or something within them withers and dies.

Mind

The playfulness of Leo can be seen most clearly in the way they engage with others, literally brightening up conversations with their optimistic mindset. Leo is creative and a mastermind at manifestation so they can dream up big scenarios, businesses, events and activities that carry that star-quality that ensures success. Leo can't be reduced to back-office thinking: they thrive on being in charge and making things happen. Their ideas are most often grand or even grandiose and others may feel they need to dial it down a bit but Leo has a knack for doing the very best, even with the least, and making it all look wonderful.

They can be bossy as Leo genuinely believes they know best and they tend to take credit for things. However, left to other people, ideas can lack the Leo lustre and it's only when Leo is involved that projects gain sparkle and get noticed. Crossing a Leo is dangerous territory so you have to pick your battles. You don't want your head bitten off by a lion on the rampage. Yet give them appreciation for their gifts and talents and you will find the collaboration works for both of you.

Body

The major organ of the heart is Leo's domain. All the connotations and connections associated with the primary pump in the body take us to the exuberant, expressive, vital warmth of Leo's big heartedness. We associate feelings and generosity with the heart itself. We talk about people having a heart of gold, or of being heartless, attributing this generosity or lack of emotion to the state of the organ itself. The heart is a huge indicator of life force and emotions as well as blood flow. The heart just keeps on giving unless it is sclerosed and diseased – and Leo as a sign is associated with all the goldeness of the heart that can be expressed out in the world and given to others.

As a Fire sign, Leo's natural energy is irrepressible and they do well with cardio exercise that keeps the organ of the heart strong and super healthy. Physical activity is important as is keeping fully engaged with life. There are lions who can lounge in their lair but they thrive on outside entertainment.

Spirit

It might seem that the confident big cat is in a permanent state of blessing and bliss. However, the Leo spirit can be crushed by indifference. There is a certain vulnerability to Leo that is not immediately obvious. Being rejected, put-down or side-lined can be traumatic for a lion whose birthright is to rise and shine. They can take a knock and later come back to centre (or centre stage), but they never forget that their success depends on the goodwill or even applause of others.

Spiritually and Karmically

Leos are here to light up our lives! It is not necessarily narcissistic to be able to generate all this heat and fire. Although, of course, there are the entitled Leos, the self-centred, suck-the-oxygen-out-of-the-room types who believe the world revolves around them and them alone. They find it hard to calibrate the way other people shrink away from them in distaste. Yet, a strong Leo pattern in a birth-chart can denote royal karma from a previous life – so it's no wonder they come in expecting to be given the star treatment.

A highly evolved Leo can use this 'royal' awareness to make other people feel special. In other words, they know how to big someone else up, make a fuss of them, create a special occasion for them and light the fire of their confidence.

Leos are here to look at life lessons around the ego. On the one hand, it is important for this sign to develop strong self-belief, self-esteem and confidence in their own abilities. On the other, this needs to be tempered by an awareness of where they fit into the larger whole and what other people have to offer.

What Does Leo Have to Give?

Without Leo, the world would be a lesser place, dimmer, more ordinary. Their capacity to ignite enthusiasm in others, to offer up that zest for life and playful creativity is a gift that helps make the world go round, increases happiness and enjoyment and ultimately can be channelled into love in all its forms.

Leo's belief in the capacity for things to manifest can plant important seeds in other people, enabling them to flourish, projects to grow, relationships to build. It is almost as if Leo can magically generate an aura that makes others feel like everything will be all right, even wonderful, if they too buy into what Leo is offering.

Perhaps Leo is extravagant, but not necessarily just for themselves. Their capacity to make someone else feel as if they too are worthy of 'only the best' can lift that person up. Leo definitely gives their fire spark out and providing it doesn't burn out of control then everyone feels better for it.

What Does Leo Need to Receive?

Praise is elixir for Leos who seriously require acknowledgement from others. Empty, ill-thought-out compliments will not hack it. Genuine appreciation is what Leo needs. After all what is the point of putting on the greatest performance of your life (and every single effort is one of those) if others do not see it, recognise it and above all enjoy it too. It is not enough for Leos to put their creative flair to use – people must be affected by it, engage with it, admire it (of course) and stand in that solar fire that has been generated by Leo for their exclusive enjoyment and entertainment. The Sun (their ruling planet) is there to make things grow and glow – so don't be a party pooper, a critic or even worse, indifferent.

However, that childlike desire to be recognised can prove exhausting for those who are short on unconditional love. Sometimes Leo needs to receive sterner stuff, to be told – if they're not already aware – that they are not the centre of the universe at all times!

What Does Leo Need to Learn?

Leo's hardest lesson is one of humility. There is a difference between being a little insecure, lacking in confidence and truly recognising that the ego is the small guy in life and the self must serve a higher purpose. Leos benefit from discovering an overview of how they might fit into the larger whole rather than dominating the proceedings, a reminder that other people's needs and choices are equally important. Ultimately Leo must learn to respect others and offer ways to enhance their lives rather than putting themselves first.

It might seem counter-intuitive, but if Leo could learn to relax into the ordinary, develop a tolerance for the simple and basic rather than the lavish and extraordinary, then many of their ego issues would reduce. Perhaps going cold turkey and exchanging the high life for street life once in a while would not only bring them down to earth, but also enhance their appreciation of the finer things as not being a right, but a blessing.

We all know that trying to obtain internal security by external means is a fruitless task. We can accumulate all the desired goods, the prize job, the trophy credentials, perfect partner, but unless we feel that internal sense of self worth nothing outside of us is ever enough to validate us. So what can Leo do to find their inner core of strength? If they give their power away to the audience then their confidence is dependent on the vagaries of the crowd. Leo can experience a far greater peace of mind from actually appreciating their own gifts and what they have to offer. In other words, a little self love can go a long way towards healing that incessant need for approval. If Leo is operating from a low level of awareness then their ego requires constant bolstering from an audience. A more evolved Leo recognises that buying into the ego is a trap, and self-love activates the power to bring joy to others.

LOVE

Dating: Love to Love You, Baby

There is no doubt that Leos are made to flirt, cavort with and pounce on the object of their desire. It can indeed feel like a cat-and-mouse game as Leo's intense interest plucks you from obscurity and forces you into a dynamic dance that can feel like a duel to the death at times. You may get the distinct feeling that you are being played, toyed with as an object of amusement. Yet Leo's romantic streak can have you entranced. Leo is so gorgeous, magnificent and so much fun that pretty soon you wonder how you ever lived a 'normal' life.

Once Leo has trained their spotlight on you, there is no turning back – at least not until the show is over, which could be one of those that runs and runs! If you date a Leo you will be treated to their idea of a good time, which usually entails the best seats in all the best places. There is absolutely nothing cheapskate about Leo. They are pure class. Nothing less will do. So you need to look the part if you are on their arm, as if to the manor born. A lion is a proud creature and they want to feel proud of you too. Making the right noises of appreciation is also important, as Leo wants to know they are hitting the spot, that you possess the taste and style that can single out the superior from the inferior.

Chancing across your big cat is made easier if you hang out at exclusive places and events. You are hardly likely to bump into them at the discount store. It helps if you have something striking about you that will captivate the Leo hunting instincts as they won't give you a second glance if you've happened out without your full dress-to-impress regalia. In fact, you need to work on your 'stand out' attributes if you want to get the lion's attention.

Once you've got them interested, if you are hoping to land a Leo, then it might be a case of no expense being spared. At the very least, an obvious effort must be made or your Leo date will lose interest. What you lack in bling may be compensated by the rare or beautiful. However, there is no point expecting your big cat to slum it. Therefore, a lot of thought has to be put into creating the right kind of experience for a Leo. Think about setting the stage with the perfect props, lighting and special effects that will bring out the best in them. Besides, you are bound to enjoy being graced by their presence, unless your nose is easily put out of joint by someone else stealing all the attention! Leos are usually great company, lively, engaging and willing to create a wonderful time. They put a brave face on their own petty sulks which tend to dispel the minute they have the distraction of the outside world. The Leo mega-watt smile can light up the room, their sheer majesty makes a normal dinner a special event. Of course, they like to talk about themselves and have some pretty amazing stories to tell – Leos have an affinity with the romantic and dramatic and are not shy when it comes to telling you all about the blaze of colour and glory in their lives together with any heroic deeds.

Yet for all their attention-seeking, Leos are just so loveable, perhaps a little in love with love but undoubtedly appreciative of and giving in all areas of romantic love. Being with them is pure gold! Intoxicating and invigorating – at least you will be living life to the full with them.

Affectionate and generous with compliments, Leos inspire love very easily and win hearts and minds with their conquering spirit. In return they expect to be worshipped and unless you are a dedicated, loyal follower who has sworn allegiance then Leo will find someone else who fits the bill. It's not that Leo wants to date a doormat. They enjoy a bit of a challenge – because it reflects on their own prowess that they have managed to corral you into their lives. You have to be special because they are special! You see nothing is allowed to be just everyday and normal in the life of the King of the Jungle. Their version of normality is somewhat rarefied so never cut corners or allow your attention to wander.

You can't expect this impressive specimen to exist without a little vanity, so cut the Leo some slack when it comes to getting ready to date you. It might be best to allow extra time for your journey and to factor in the way Leos will often arrive late anyway in order to make an entrance and to guarantee the theatre is ready for them. Once you get the hang of being with royalty you'll recognise that your job is to ensure everything runs smoothly and that your lion never has to encounter transport difficulties, mislaid bookings or, heaven forbid, less-than-excellent quality in anything. You may have to raise your standards to match theirs – but isn't that a good thing?

You may also have to suck it up when Leo overrules your own preferences. Because, of course, they know best! Wherever you have been, they have done it better, so why compete? You should be grateful for their superior know-how, in Leo's book at least. And if you aren't then perhaps you would be better off dating an insecure Libra or Pisces who will say yes to everything you want. It takes some inner substance in order to handle Leo – a recognition that you are not diminished in any way by their presence, but rather enhanced by it. Even if you get things wrong and Leo moves into overbearing mode, then it helps to recognise that they are only trying to make things better. Even if they make them worse!

Leos make ardent lovers and having wooed you with lavish tokens of love they will set about making you feel like a prince or princess in the bedroom. Don't forget this is a sparky Fire sign, so enthusiasm for physical combustion is a must. Affection and grooming gestures are also appreciated in both private and public. The lion loves to have you in his or her paws or to be demonstrably worshipped by you.

Treat your Leo as if you are dating a superstar – because you are! Leo doesn't do compliant or second best and as long as you look up to them, respect them and maintain their dignity you will feel as if you have been given the secret code to the sphinx!

Keeping the Big Cat in Captivity

If you are moving towards forming a lion's pride with your Leo then it's best to go in with your eyes open. Leos have a natural instinct for heading up the family, taking care of their cubs and still maintaining their position as King of the Jungle. What happens when you try to confine your cat to captivity is another matter! You will soon get a caged lion on your hands, prowling up and down, snarling and being driven demented unless it can be the beautiful roaming lion it was born to be. If you get into that tango of trying to be a lion tamer then it might not work out well for either of you. It's always best to maintain the feeling of freedom for your lion, even if it is to all intents and purposes an illusion. The big cat likes to think that it is entirely their choice to stay with you.

If you are having wedding nuptials, then your lion will obviously want to make it a big splash of an occasion – it is a royal wedding after all! The event itself will be one enormous showstopper as no other sign can create the wow factor like Leo.

Living with Leo will transform any home into a castle. It is a case of needs must, so opulence is the name of the game, even if it is discreetly so. Your shared lair will be a perpetual show home, even if no one is coming over. However, Leo likes to entertain and show off a bit, so when people are invited it is likely to be the full five-star treatment rather than a slap-up kitchen supper.

Keeping everything in top-notch condition is important for Leo and they need a lot of lion-like pampering themselves, especially when it comes to the Leo mane, which requires a lot of maintenance in order to create the desired look.

Once settled with a Leo you can rest assured you are the 'chosen one' and your job in life is simply to create your pussycat purr with delight in your company and make your lives together. For Leo, having a lovely time with each other is all that matters. Yes, there will be times when their way of making you feel subservient grates. But you must always understand that Leo is much more fragile than they appear and they are, in fact, totally dependent on your love and support.

The lion is the one who will always be front of house in the union. They will be head honcho, chief greeter and CEO, so don't make unilateral decisions – they see it as an affront to their dignity. On the other hand, they think nothing of making decisions without consulting you. Your choice here is whether you want to be with them or not. Which is why it's always important to know what you're letting yourself in for in the first place. When you sign up to be with a Leo you are basically entering into a benevolent dictatorship! It's not for everyone, but if it floats your boat and you can keep your own sense of perspective and confidence, it can be a sunny partnership.

Together you could conquer the world, as long as you let Leo do the conquering. They won't let you forget that you are lucky to be on the A-team and also the A-list for that matter!

Leo is loyal by nature, as long as they are receiving enough attention. Take your eyes off them and shower compliments on other people and they visibly wilt. Just saying!

You get the drill with Leo, know how to keep your lion and your marriage in tip-top condition. What you receive in return is beyond measure, for Leo can literally put you on top of the world and you receive all the love from that fabulous heart chakra of theirs.

The Ex Factor: Excommunication and Exile

Leo is fizzy like champagne and a sure sign that something is wrong is when their bubbly nature goes flat. The light within dims, they begin to lose their sparkle in your presence. This is a warning sign that something is badly wrong.

The dangers inherent in a partnership with Leo are fairly obvious. You might feel trampled on, or have a low tolerance for what you perceive as their self-centredness or arrogance. Their overbearing ways could have got too much. Perhaps you grew tired of being the satellite of the Sun King or Queen and are ready to move within your own orbit. Having had to maintain such high standards of excellence, perhaps you are longing to kick back, relax and chill out.

A spurned Leo is a spitting cat. They find it hard to forgive betrayal and disloyalty. Don't expect to be friends with Leo once they have got their claws out. You might become prey or sworn enemies. The most you can hope for is a safe distance, providing you show contrition and respect. Leo will draw a circle around themselves and their lives from which you will be excluded.

The sudden exile makes it feel as if the Sun has fallen from the sky. A bitter chill descends – you might even find yourself missing the life you are dropped from. You may no longer be welcome at Court, but you got your own life back. Adjusting to being a commoner rather than a consort takes time but from a safe distance you can savour having all that energy for YOU again.

If Leo is the one who walks away from you, then you might be lucky enough to be treated with a generous retainer. A pay-off that is commensurate with your years of duty and homage. Leo is rarely stingy or mean. It simply doesn't suit them. Unless, of course, the division of spoils results in a huge dent in their own lifestyle which would hit them hard. If you want to keep your Leo on side then do not reduce them to a meagre existence.

Leos are proud parents of their offspring and their playful nature is reignited around children, so your Leo ex will most probably continue to shine as a parent even if your own relationship with them has died. It is a little reminder of the good times . . .

DESTINY

The Leo Entourage and Glossy Posse

Leos absolutely must be leaders. At any event, in any photograph, Leo can switch it on and steal the show, leaving everyone else in the background. It's almost as if the best camera angles and flattering lighting are always set up for them and then they just leap into the front and click. It's all about them, even if it's your party! Leo is the one you would definitely pick out of the crowd.

However, a Leo friend is usually the warmest person in your team or tribe. You can look forward to their being there as everything suddenly lights up and the fun begins. A guaranteed good time is in store and Leo can lift the mood in the room like no one else.

The kinds of people in the lion's pride are those who luxuriate in being royally chosen and are not going to compete for the top spot.

Leo obviously needs worker bees as a supporting act and hopefully wouldn't take ALL the credit for what you did. The practical, mundane aspects of pulling together a project is usually delegated to those who can handle service to others. Leo instinctively knows this isn't their remit. It is your job to do the washing up, theirs to create a spectacular soirée or whatever it happens to be.

Yet if you have a lion in your midst, you will look back on some of your own biggest occasions and realise that it was Leo who knew exactly how to make you feel special at that time, how to put the whole thing together so that it sparkled. Really you should be grateful! And if you aren't, then your Leo will certainly make their displeasure felt and maybe cast you adrift.

Socially, Leos enjoy the grand events – the ones with cachet and style where they can see and be seen. You have to put on your best bib and tucker and add value to the occasion and look as if you love it all as much as they do.

As Leo gravitates towards jobs which also involve some kind of prestigious angle, if you are part of their team you must show a high degree of pizzazz and style. It all reflects on them! They are the best after all. And that means if you are with them, then you must be too.

LEO

♌

ALTAR OBJECTS

Place some of these objects on your altar or carry them with you in actual or pictorial form.

*

CRYSTAL: tourmaline, topaz, amber, chrysolite

MINERAL/METAL: gold

LEO SYMBOLS: the lion, heart shapes

TAROT CARDS: The Sun, Strength

ANGEL CARDS: Angel Verchiel, Archangel Raziel

FLOWERS: sunflowers, illawarra flame tree

TREE: cypress

SCENTS OR CANDLES: citrus: lemongrass, neroli, lime, mandarin, lemon balm, melissa

MEMORY BOARD/PHOTOGRAPHS/PICTURES: theatre tickets, photographs of special occasions, film stars; painting: 'Sunflowers' by Vincent Van Gogh

CLOTH: gold silk or brocade

TALISMAN: Apollo the Sun God, the Sun, bees

*

VIRGO

VIRGO

Veracity and Virtue

♍

CORE QUALITIES: *deliberate, thoughtful, refined, realistic, anxious*

Mantra: I silence the inner critic as everything is perfect, just as it is.

The constellation of Virgo: Virgo is the second largest constellation in the sky and the largest constellation in the zodiac. It lies between Leo to the west and Libra to the east. Its brightest star is Spica.

Virgo resembles slightly sparkling water. Not too effervescent and showy, but unmistakeably alert and alive. They are not the obvious hit-you-between-the-eyeballs type, so you have to look for them, notice them, as much as they are quietly observing you. Which they are. In fact, it can get a bit uncomfortable under a Virgo's unrelenting gaze as you just know that they have spotted the missing button that came off, the slightly scuffed shoe. They may not say anything, but it is all being taken in and noted. Because Virgo does not want to miss a trick. It is their big fear, that something has slipped through their discrimination system and observatory. You see, they don't want to be caught out. Virgo is nobody's fool and realises that most people miss things. Their gift is for noticing the one thing that no one else saw – the fly in the ointment that has to be dealt with in order to meet exacting standards. Yes, Virgo has the highest of expectations. They may not impose their criteria or quality control on you but you will quickly see that they have raised the concept of making a choice into an art form. One of the soul lessons of Virgo is to live with the less-than-perfect. For them, this is a tall order.

Of course, if you want a job done properly then ask a Virgo. They are the ones who will toil away, unflinchingly, long after the lightweights have given up. For Virgo it is not a matter of soaking up praise and recognition – in fact, Virgo considers these qualities flimsy; they are seeking material perfection that is built to last.

As an Earth sign, Virgo has a natural affinity with all that is solid, tangible and real. They have a hands-on approach to life and can get things done with minimum fuss and error. Not for them the endless fantasies and distractions that occupy those with grandiose visions. Virgo works with the doable and viable. Yet, they are also ruled by the mind-planet Mercury which gives them the edge when it comes to strategy and putting ideas together.

Virgo is essentially a gentle soul. Their 'virgin' moniker belies their sensuality, but what they do possess is a desire for goodness. The whole idea of sin, purity and redemption is a matter that occupies Virgo either consciously or unconsciously. Sometimes, they play on both fields – almost to fully experience the worst of human nature in order to get a handle on its purification. Virgo itself is not immune to behaving as badly as any other sign. But they are more likely to beat themselves up for it if they feel they have wronged or harmed someone. That is unless they have jumped right over to the chaotic, addictive, lost-soul energy inherent in Pisces – the polarity at the other end of their axis.

What Virgo has to offer is a cool head in a crisis and the kindness to give you exactly what you need in your hour of need (this sign regards lack of punctuality as a criminal offence). Virgo is undeniably a giver – of advice, practical help – and a purveyor of resources that can be called upon. Their finely formed intellect and fount of knowledge makes them incredibly good at solving problems. Anything from riddles to right old messes. They are also reasonable – which is a plus if you like that kind of thing. Some people find them just a little too immersed in the world of reason and perhaps a little cynical when it comes to matters of the heart.

LIFE

Health

Well, this is Virgo's specialist subject. Many visitors to Virgo's abode find cupboards full of vitamins and vials of freshly picked herbs which they combine with their matcha or juice-fast ingredients. Most Virgos learn to watch what they eat. This is because many suffer from nervous indigestion and a sensitive gut that simply can't handle overload.

Mind

Virgo has one of the most active minds on the planet. These Mercury-ruled, mutable types are constantly engaged in researching, analysing and defining information and answers. It is a habit they can't break – even if it's 4 a.m. With the advent of the smart phone and constant access to all the mind-stuff, Virgos find it extremely hard to switch off. Even if they remove all technology from their bedroom, their mind is whirring with downloads of thoughts that require processing and which keep them awake at night. Repetitive thinking is an issue, as is worry. The negative meditation of worry is Virgo's bugbear, partly because they cannot help wondering about all the what ifs. Their tendency to overthink makes them their own worst enemy.

They are brilliant at synthesising information and can argue points without getting heated or losing their place. Astute and clever, Virgo is the person who thinks of everything and is also ready to ask the necessary pertinent question. What's more, Virgo will actually listen to your answer – a rare quality and a very important one in terms of keeping lines of communication open. There are the chatty Virgos who are never short of words, always able to find common ground, and those who are more of the silent type, carefully paying attention before uttering their well-thought-out analysis. Either way, you will find Virgo thought-provoking and stimulating company.

Body

Virgo is associated with all the fine workings of the digestive process. Both bodily and in life, Virgo connects with assimilation, sorting and sifting, breaking down raw components and assigning them to perfect order. It is the area of the intestines and stomach which tends to give Virgo trouble as a sure sign that 'something is not quite right'. It seems that emotional facets of life that are indigestible to Virgo end up leaving their toll on the gut.

Virgos do not easily carry excess weight, they tend towards being wiry and lean and everything about them looks quite neat, as if they were cut out of a catalogue. This is not just surface appearance either. Virgo pays attention to all parts of the body – so personal hygiene rates highly and they generally know how to take care of themselves with the help of endless rituals that create bespoke rhythms to their day. The everyday accoutrements Virgo carry about their person can be items as varied as a tongue-scraper, Swiss army knife or homeopathic Nux Vomica (to settle that tummy trouble).

Spirit

As the saying goes, cleanliness is next to godliness, and it seems as though clean-living, eco-friendly Virgo has it all licked. Yet, the finely tuned nervous system of Virgo can wreak havoc with their spirit in terms of balance and wellbeing. Virgo is a mutable sign, never standing still for long and constantly changing mental permutations so that they are in a never-ending whirr. It means that Virgo finds it hard to relax, to really let go. In fact, this art has to be learned as Virgo feels they should be doing something purposeful and useful at all times. Of course, if they translate this as filling their day with the minutiae of tasks, they will be busy but actually distracted from their real soul purpose. Which is relatively simple – they are here to serve. But this can be translated into a much bigger picture, rather than reducing the idea of service to waiting on people hand and foot.

Spiritually and Karmically

Virgo is here to sort the wheat from the chaff. Their purification process is second to none and they are on the path of discernment. However, too much of this meticulous checking can lead to such duality between good or bad, right or wrong that they will be on a lifelong search to find their holy grail of perfection. Undeniably, Virgos are hard to please because they are built to reject and refine. They can't reach all-encompassing undifferentiated states – such as love – very easily! Perhaps they need to learn how to discriminate in this lifetime; too much attachment to every little thing can result in finicky behaviour.

What Does Virgo Have to Give?

As natural givers, Virgos are leaned on quite a bit by those who can't get their act together. Yet Virgo also needs to receive, to delegate, to let others do something for them.

Virgos orchestrate the little details in the environment that make life palatable for others and their fussing over whether it is the right temperature, whether you have had your 5-a-day, whether it might rain and you should take an umbrella, is perfectly sweet but unless you believe in the God of small things alone, perhaps it's a waste of their considerable powers to only focus on the minor things; to not use their considerable energy for doing good in the world.

Without Virgo, other people would have to clean up and take responsibility. Virgo's selflessness means that they are often taken for granted in their everyday endeavours to stem the tide of chaos. Humble by nature, they do not seek credit but there is no doubt that they can be overlooked or trampled over by those eager for the glittering prizes.

Virgo's perfectionism means that they will work hard at doing something very well. They do not believe in things being handed to them on a plate. Their efficiency, organisational skills and capable approach are a form of dedication that is often underrated in this throwaway, instant-results world. Their mastery of physical forms can be channelled into areas as diverse as sexuality or producing incredible food – but they really do enjoy giving pleasure to others.

What Does Virgo Need to Receive?
Because Virgo can be so cool, almost detached in their modus operandi, they do need warming up! They may shrug their shoulders if you praise them, but secretly they are delighted that their efforts did not go to waste. They will never admit it, but Virgos are often drawn to more creative, chaotic, emotional types because that sort of magnetic energy appeals to Virgo's uptightness. They need to be loosened from their own interminable mental machinations and just be. Yes, to BE is an unnatural state for Virgo,

but a valuable one for them to experience. Freedom from having to be get things right generates peace of mind.

Virgo's tendency to criticise and carp can be irritating for those of a sunnier disposition. They are predisposed to think negatively about what could go wrong, the downside. This is why they do well around people who exude a 'bright side' energy and who can balance faults and failings with fun and frivolity.

The practice of gratitude can be very healing for Virgo, who often fixates on what is wrong.

What Does Virgo Need to Learn?

As Virgo is essentially such a careful type, they are actually repelled by wastefulness and carelessness. This is all very laudable, but at times this sign could do with being more spontaneous and discovering that the sky doesn't fall in as a result. As everything has to be 'the real thing', Virgo sometimes misses out on the fun of simply going along for the ride and not expecting too much. For Virgo to allow themselves the magic of going with the flow, the excitement of the surprise is truly a wonderful thing. It recaptures a childlike playfulness that changes their energy from dry and dutiful, to fun-loving and free.

The maxim 'no one is perfect' is something Virgo needs to grasp. Allowing others to have their faults and not judging them for it is a big release. Of course, Virgo can't help noticing when you've got it wrong, but if they can turn the other cheek it raises their frequency. The caricature nagging shrew Virgo is only activated under extreme stress. When Virgo is able to find the confidence to believe in themselves, they can be so magnificent that they can achieve the Eastern mindset of everything being, no matter what (and even more so if it patently isn't), perfect!

As Virgo unravels their tightly woven agenda, being prepared for every eventuality and protected against every germ, emotion or sudden about-turn, they can literally drop into the terra firma of being held in existence without the need for it all to be such a big deal.

LOVE

Dating Vestal Virgin Virgo

Virgos get a bad rap in the dating stakes with their name implying a prudishness that is far from the case. In ancient times the virgin goddesses of the temple performed sacred rites. Vestal virgins undertook a vow of chastity but were thought to be the embodiment of Roman society.

As an Earth sign, Virgo is very much in touch with the body and the senses and takes great pleasure in both. But there is nothing obvious about Virgo – they are discreet and refined so they are not going to walk around displaying their wares to all and sundry. There is also nothing slapdash or slung together about Virgo, who conveys a well-groomed look.

Virgo won't flirt indiscriminately (or even at all if the truth be known!). You see, they are for real and have no time for false compliments, fake intimacy and fatuous flings. That is not to say that Virgo lacks playfulness – but it is through the mind that you can reach Virgo. Virgo feels attraction through the *idea* of you. Whilst you are busy answering their twenty questions, Virgo is building up a dossier, designed to inform them of whether you are worth their time and effort or not. The Virgo dating style is a masterclass in risk management. It can be pretty disconcerting to feel that you are a research project. You are not receiving the right vibes that tell you any sparks are flying. However, the extraordinary thing is that just as you have convinced yourself that Virgo does not have any desire for you, that you have failed the test by some petty misdemeanour and therefore you're going to be just friends in a purely cerebral way, they will pounce. Then you find out just how non-virginal Virgo can be!

The mind and the body are the big hooks for Virgo – the way in.

What they fear most, the place they are least comfortable, is the realm of the heart. Virgo does not trust feelings as they place their faith in mental and physical qualities. For a start, they have no wish to be out of control and emotions are likely to destabilise the smooth running of their world. As Virgo readily represses their feelings, keeping them contained and cool, it isn't easy to gauge where things are going. They text you and talk to you, they appraise you and transmit physical attraction but where is their heart? This is the question you need to ask Virgo, sooner or later. Surprisingly, if you open up this topic you will find that Virgo is lost here, doesn't have an answer, doesn't really know how they feel – it is all about what they think or what their body tells them. So, dating a Virgo can be a minefield for those that function on a feeling level. The temptation is to fill in Virgo's gaps for them, make allowances for their 'busy schedules' and to polarise with them by keeping your heart open whilst theirs is marked 'no entry'. Yet this is really doing a disservice to Virgo, who needs to move into emotional engagement, actually dare to live in their heart and give feelings equal billing to the mind.

So, if you're dating a Virgo, get ready to be analysed and recognise that, as time is of the essence for them, the mere fact they are bestowing some of this valuable commodity on you is a compliment. That is, if you ever get to see them, because Virgo is always working late, has a million things to do and absolutely everything else is always going to be more important than matters of the heart.

In fact, it can be quite hard to actually meet a Virgo unless you chance upon them at work or in the course of performing any number of useful things. Internet dating is a great time-saving device for them as they can keep you at a safe distance and put you through their processor (alongside many others). You may in fact see little of them.

It might seem that Virgo is a dating nightmare yet once you have earned their trust you will find there is no one more considerate, tender or winsome than Virgo. If you want a flashy type, full of hearts, flowers and romance then look elsewhere. What you get with Virgo is something else altogether, something more real.

Always remember that although Virgo seems emotionally contained, underneath they are sensitive, almost nervy, with wiring that can quickly unravel – although they try to keep this under wraps. If you read their aura you can see the jumpiness there and the little particles of emotional and nervous energy dancing around. It can be a strange experience looking at all the movement in their energy field whilst Virgo insists, with a straight face, that everything is 'absolutely fine'.

When Virgos do decide you are worth it, they will make plans to see you. Not for them the spontaneous, 'Hey, shall we grab a drink somewhere?'. The date will be carefully calculated and orchestrated and commensurate with their rating of you. Similarly, if you are thinking of romancing a Virgo it is wise to give them plenty of advance warning and to leave nothing to chance.

Get them onto safe ground, as Virgo is actually quite shy, even though they can be talkative if you find the kind of topics that interest them and provide a vehicle for expressing opinions rather than feelings. It is best not to take them out of their physical comfort zone either – an environment such as karaoke or the ice skating rink could expose them to mishap – which is Virgo's bête noir.

Virgos possess a magnetic attraction because they are almost always very well put together and their earthy sensuality is evident just a little beneath their highly alert intelligence. The fertility goddess that is Virgo's symbol has a natural affinity with cultivating and procreating. As some signs might try to laugh you into bed, Virgo will talk you into it so that you might in the end have no arguments left with which to resist! Once there, you will realise that Virgo is the sign of technique and skill. Perhaps not passionate abandonment, but a lover who understands that union is more than just a physical act. Whilst Virgo may carry a certain germ-phobic, neat-nick way about them, what they long for is the end of all that separation and division and to experience the magic of being able to truly merge with another.

Timing is everything with Virgo – they will rarely step outside of their time-managed lives to create space for you if it clashes with other things they feel they need to do. They are not above making you wait for what they consider to be the right moment. Appropriateness is another issue – they find it hard to take a risk on someone who doesn't tick their clearly defined box, doesn't conform to their idea of how things should be and, more importantly, how YOU should be. The pursuit of Mr or Mrs Right is something Virgo takes very seriously, yet, despite their heavy vetting, they often end up making 'mistakes' – simply because they are human, after all.

However, if you make it past their internal judgement panel, you will find that Virgo is a great date. You can really talk to them which makes everything more enjoyable. Pretty soon you will wonder how you ever lived without running everything by them.

Keeper of the Sacred Flame

If you're thinking of taking things to the next level with Virgo, rest assured that this sign actually understands how to 'make things work'. This is because smooth running matters to them. They enjoy fixing problems and finding solutions – and, of course, in any marriage or long-term union there will be a glitch in the hitch. Those vestal virgins were guardians of the flame and tasked with ensuring the sacred fire never went out. In marriage, Virgo will do everything possible to ensure the same.

Virgos have a paradoxical attitude to big events. Namely, they desire not to make the occasion into too much of a fuss or to draw attention to themselves, whilst being inherently fussy over every little thing. Their flair for co-ordination means that their plans should unfold as envisaged (and will be double checked over and over again!).

Once you've signed on the dotted line with a Virgo (either in deed or written across your hearts) don't think that your Virgo partner will give up at the first sign of trouble. On the contrary, they are unswerving in their devotion to the cause. Even though they may be criticising you under their breath (if you're lucky) or more vocally (if not), they are fundamentally dedicated to the task in hand. Now, that might not sound romantic – but when all is said and done, commitment requires serious effort and this sign is unstinting in terms of putting a lot in. Their forte is the finesse they apply to the task in hand, their striving for excellence, so for some signs Virgo is literally the perfect consort.

Your Virgo partner might be picky about the way you hang the towels, or stack the dishwasher, but they are usually kind-hearted. They have their own little habits and rituals which might drive you crazy, as if they are slightly OCD, even if they're not. Yet, you can grow fond of their ways, which are designed to ward off evil. Evil to Virgo is impending chaos in any form and they will do everything in their power to guard against it.

Of course, there are some Virgos who are such sticklers for perfection that anyone who lives with them is going to be subject to constant criticism or nagging. Inevitably, Virgo's partner will fall short at times and this is when Virgo should ask themselves whether their incessant fault-finding is counter-productive to a match made in heaven.

The tidiness issue is one that causes trouble in many Virgo households. Virgos are known to never run out of anything because the replacement is always to be found lined up behind the one in use. Such efficiency can run a home like clock-work, but people are not machines and Virgo finds the emotional nuances of relationships to be an untidy irritant. Pretty soon, the partner begins to feel misunderstood.

Then there is the martyr Virgo partner, the 'what can I do for you' type who is constantly running around performing jobs. They claim that it is easier to do everything themselves but underneath the resentment builds and the carping becomes increasingly passive-aggressive.

However, if Virgo can let go a bit, allow themselves to relax into the union, then a mutually supportive partnership is made. Virgo is considerate and thoughtful and won't forget the small things that make the world go round. They are there for you and you can have a partnership that is not just functioning, or going through the motions, but of very high quality. Virgo usually shows they care through practical means instead of wearing their heart on their sleeve, but you will be left in no doubt that they are seriously invested in you. If you have got as far as the altar with Virgo you know they've really thought about it. You must have something very special together to have come this far.

With Virgo as your partner you will always be given assistance by them. They will try their hardest to give you what you need, to do what you asked and to support you. Isn't this the best kind of devotion? Trying is very important in Virgo's books. They will make an effort and expect you to make one too. Together you can be a great team.

The Ex Factor: Done and Dusted

If you've come to the end of the road with Virgo you have probably already exhausted all possibilities as Virgo would never leave something half undone. Clear-eyed Virgo, the most cynical and realistic of signs, can reach a point where they have nothing left to give. If they are the ones doing the leaving, you will be given a thorough break-down of what went wrong. They will have already spent a great deal of time working out all the weak spots, flaws and failings and after extensive analysis come up with the conclusion that your partnership simply cannot be mended.

As Virgo slips back into their aloof manner, dissecting the death of this union as if they are in the science lab, you must remind yourself that you were never with a great romantic in the first place. So, it's hardly surprising that they are so cool, unsentimental and matter-of-fact at this stage. You are now surplus to requirements – simple as that.

If you are the one who is splitting from your Virgo then you are going to be dealing with an injured soul, no doubt about it.

Virgo finds it almost impossible to comprehend that 'after everything I've done for you, the sacrifices I've made, you could do this to me'. You had better have a very good reason. As reason is the only thing that will make any sense to them. A Virgo who is left behind can be catapulted into feelings they have kept at bay for years. It can be a cathartic experience, but inevitably involves a very steep learning curve.

When it comes to carving up the resources, Virgo is the supreme mathematician, attending to every detail and arguing every point. In keeping with their controlled nature, there is unlikely to be much drama. However, don't expect to get away with anything.

Virgo is a responsible, dedicated parent and will remember every occasion and important event and also come up trumps with the finer details. They may split hairs over timing and arrangements, but ultimately they wish to be a force for good.

DESTINY

The Virgo A-Team

Virgo is an excellent team-player because they are pre-disposed to seeing how things fit together. Great at dispensing with hangers-on (Virgo feels everyone must have a purpose), they will assign each person a specific task, a job description – this goes for work too!

Seriously, if you want to be on Virgo's A-team you are expected to pull your weight and to perform your assignation to the best of your ability. Virgo is a consummate professional, never off-duty.

Their social tribe is culled from those that operate across a wide variety of interests. This way Virgo can keep their fingers on lots of tabs. Virgo might be the chief organiser, the chairman or the cleaner, but they are always humble, not given to huge displays of ego or excess. They know everyone is of value. This is where Virgo excels: positioning. They can always see your niche.

They are always understated, brandishing their to-do list and running a constant reality check. Yet when the tangibles get tangled no one is better than Virgo at unpicking the knot. They perform good works, follow instructions to the letter and know where, why and how every tiny interconnected cog in the wheel fits together. Always on time, reliable and discreet. Come to think of it – wouldn't you want them on your own team?

VIRGO

♍

ALTAR OBJECTS

Place some of these objects on your altar or carry them with you in actual or pictorial form.

*

CRYSTAL: citrine, celestite, fluorite

MINERAL/METAL: mercury

VIRGO SYMBOL: Madonna

TAROT CARD: The Hermit

ANGEL CARDS: Angel Hamaliel, Archangel Metatron

FLOWERS: marigold, carnation, pansy

TREE: cedar

SCENTS AND CANDLES: vanilla, vetiver, lavender, wood

MEMORY BOARD/PHOTOGRAPHS/PICTURES: lists, landscapes, natural objects e.g. conkers, acorns; painting: 'Madonna and Child' by Benozzo Gozolli

CLOTH: linen in taupe or natural colour

TALISMAN: mercury

*

LIBRA

LIBRA

What is Fair in Love and War?

CORE QUALITIES: *peace seeker, people person, lover of beauty, indecisive, relationship orientated*

Mantra: Today I will return to my centre without the need for other people's approval.

The constellation of Libra: Libra lies between Virgo to the west and Scorpio to the east. It is visible during a Northern Hemisphere summer, yet it doesn't have any first magnitude stars, making it fairly faint.

Libra is allegedly the most romantic sign on the planet. However, there is romance of the mind and that of the heart and as Libra is a mentally oriented Air sign, they are perhaps more in love with the *idea* of love than its translation into actual feelings and experience, when things can get messy.

Libra is primarily identified with the realm of thinking and they are capable of thinking many beautiful thoughts, building castles in the air and philosophising on the importance of love in human interaction. They can wax lyrical on how people should give to each other, be fair in their dealings, harmonious and agreeable. Yet the everyday business of relating can be a rude awakening for those born under this sign.

People do tend to flock around Libra as they are so socially skilled and charming. They draw others to them with their special combination of sweetness and light, appreciative and personable nature. What's not to like? Well, when you get into the one-to-one arena with Libra this is where the union of opposites takes hold and you start to experience the polarization that Libra manifests. Some of them are quite capable of hooking you with honey and turning into Marmite pretty quickly! How does this happen? Well, Libra needs an opposite in order to know who they are. They bounce off you and therefore you find yourself cast into the role of 'other' as being everything that Libra does not identify with. You are the yin to their yang, the black to their white – Libra needs to have two scales with which to measure, and move towards, balance.

Libra proclaims that they want harmony, yet they are always looking for the other side of the story or the argument. If you expected Libra to take your side, well, think again as they are virtually incapable of doing that without examining the counter point of view.

Yet, they do a good job of maximising beautiful surroundings and experiences as they possess a great flair for creating elegance due to their affinity with the goddess Aphrodite. Librans look as though they have been painted by Botticelli and they adore the attractions of artistry and feminine energy, no matter which sex they are. It is almost as though they believe that if everything looks serene and pleasing to the eye, then all discord will be kept at bay.

Many Librans express dismay that their lives do not seem harmonious or balanced, yet as with every Sun sign, they are on the path towards their desired attributes. These attributes were not always downloaded at birth. In fact, it is very important for Libra to realise that they are *striving* towards achieving a balance and all manner of lopsided experiences are destined along the way.

Libra is a people pleaser par excellence and they generally find themselves high-up in the popularity stakes with many likes. Yet even Libra eventually discovers that trying to be all things to all people leads to an increasingly smaller sense of personal satisfaction. Sometimes Libra simply doesn't know what they really want, think or feel because everything has been diluted by other people's opinions and output.

LIFE

Health

Libra's agreeable presence may bring out the best in others but it all takes a toll on this sign's capacity to be true to self, to express self and to have a healthy relationship with self. Whilst peace and harmony reign on the surface, scratch it and you will find niggling resentments that have gone underground, thereby blocking up the flow between mind, body and spirit and severely impacting Libra's delicate balance.

Mind

As befits an Air sign, Libra possesses a brilliance in terms of connecting abstract ideas, facts and even figures. Their penchant for perfect symmetry comes in handy for presenting both sides of the argument, making comparisons and collating contradictory information. Libra combines a politician's mind with a diplomat's spin, thereby creating thought forms that make such a pleasant impression that the listener is disarmed. Libra uses this as a negotiation tactic. They are strategists and will offer up the give so that they bag what they want to take.

Of course, few people realise they are also being used as a vital sounding board whilst Libra weighs up every pro and con before a decision can be reached. Famously indecisive, those born under the sign of the scales enjoy debating rather than decision-making. They have a horror of getting it wrong, of offending people and will avoid making irrevocable choices whenever possible.

Body

The kidneys are the area of the body associated with Libra. Two kidneys denote the perfect pairing of Libra's make-up and their function of filtration also correlates to Libra as they act as a place where the 'bad' is expelled and the goodness retained. The kidneys are also resonant with the idea of stress in Chinese medicine. Longevity is thought to be held in the amount of jing essence stored in the kidneys which is weakened by the hormones of adrenaline and cortisol. Fear is an emotion that draws on the reserves in the kidneys. Keeping a balance, experiencing peace and harmony is central to Libra's wellbeing.

As Libra is wholly identified with looking good, their general appearance and presentation is usually stylish and elegant. They are often particularly blessed in the looks department and their energy is likeable, never loud and abrasive.

Spirit

As Libra depends so much on other people's approval, their spirit can be easily affected by what they receive and how they are regarded. Libra is looking for smiles. Their raison d'etre is to 'get on with other people' and they cannot deal with ugly scenes or emotions. They view lack of manners as a huge defect, because in Libra's world of politeness and etiquette everyone should operate from a place of appreciation. Manners make Libra's world go round and certainly smooths their own path as they go to great lengths to ensure people are thanked and treated with respect.

Spiritually and Karmically

Librans promote co-operation. They are skilled at resolving differences and keeping people happy. Their gift for keeping the peace means that many warring factions can co-exist. Libra possesses the neutrality of Switzerland. No mean feat when all around them people might be at loggerheads and operating on a dog-eat-dog policy. Being with a Libra helps other signs to remember the concept of fairness. That there are two sides to any story and that opposing forces can be reconciled.

Libra is quintessentially the sign of the relationship. Their ruling planet is Venus, goddess of love, and all that she represents in terms of pleasing others, engaging in partnerships and appreciating all things beautiful. Venus may be a planet associated with love, but in ancient times she was also a major player in war. Let us not forget the Trojan War was triggered by the goddess Venus (Aphrodite) demanding a choice. The Mayans also timed sending their troops into war to coincide with the exact moment Venus ended her retrograde cycle. Her resonance with strategy can be used in both love and war and could best be symbolised as a kind of art of war for lovers.

What Does Libra Have to Give?
Libra keeps us focused on the idea of love and whatever it may mean to each of us. An inherently civilised sign, Libra draws us away from the reptilian limbic brain where predators tear each other to shreds, and towards a courteous, gentler realm where we consider other people's needs. Libra is about chivalry, fairness and equality. Perhaps everything is not always as fair in love and war as Libra would like, but this sign helps us to step back from going all out for ourselves.

Perhaps Libra's idealistic approach is a million miles away from most people's reality, but without Libra we would live in an even pushier world. Libra's lifelong desire is to take a moment to smell the roses, to inject a little romance into our time here on planet

Earth and above all that people should be 'nice' to each other. Not such a bad thing! Single-handedly this sign creates the ambient lighting and romantic settings that soften the hard edges in life.

What Does Libra Need to Receive?

If we consider where Libra is positioned on the spectrum of transmitting and receiving they are placed at the far end of receiving simply because they only see who they are in relation to another person. Therefore, whenever they are in a relationship with another it makes a huge impact on them. It is an irony that this sign of balance and equality is so frequently put out of kilter by the strong presence of a partner or a significant other.

Libra needs people – even if it is in the form of a sparring partner, a tennis partner, an other half, a significant other. Yet Libra will create a relationship with anyone: as soon as they show up at the coffee shop, for instance, they are engaged in human interaction and are aware of the energy exchange with the other person, even if it doesn't go beyond the social niceties. So, if you meet a Libra, know that you are entering the duo state of being, the dance of mirroring, reflection, opposites attracting, exchanging, all of the intricacies of two humans interacting.

What Does Libra Need to Learn?

It is one of Libra's great disappointments to discover that life really is not fair. It contains so many ups and downs, sudden about-turns, surprise disasters and miracles that it resembles more a game of snakes and ladders than a perfectly apportioned set of experiences designed to give us all equal billing. Some Librans might wonder what they have done in a previous life to deserve their 'bad hand', but once they elevate their perspective they come to realise that no one has it all. There are degrees, of course, there are good things that happen to bad people and vice versa, leaving Libra scratching their head and wondering what, if any, the rules of life really are and whether there is any justice? Justice is something that bothers Libra, even keeping them awake at night. Yet we simply cannot know why certain things happen; it is part of the mystery of life. As Libra can offset some of life's darkness through their endeavour for fair play to prevail, for beauty to shine through, for love to matter, they are most certainly doing their bit to keep the Venus energy flowing. They have a role to play here which is very important.

If Libra pushes the shadow realm away, refusing to acknowledge it, then the shadow gains power and grows bigger. Sometimes Libra has to acknowledge that the meaner side of human nature has more power if it is never addressed. Avoiding conflict is not always the answer and can in fact escalate differences. Libra stands in their strength if they can look difficulties in the eye rather than air-brushing them out. Glossing over the facts may make everything look pretty, but it doesn't convey the absolute truth.

If Libra can dare to speak their own mind, without first ascertaining what everyone else thinks and adjusting themselves accordingly, then they can bring more to any relationship. The Shangri-la of perfect harmony is an illusion that keeps Libra on a tightrope of a balancing act, when in fact it might be a masterstroke to simply agree to disagree.

LOVE

Dating: Libra in Love with Love

Libra is a big flirt and easily able to win you over with their charm offensive, perfectly lovely demeanour and engaging interest in you. If your path crosses with a Libra, you are instantly drawn into the possibility of meeting your match. Because Libra is always looking to see how you might fit together. If single, they seek their other half, as they are predisposed to coupledom and have an aversion to being on their own. So Libra will assess you, start measuring out the proportions of who you are, compared to who they are. Libra is looking for a perfect union of things in common and poles apart so that there is a balance, an even proportion of qualities between you.

It can feel very flattering to be the object of their interest and they are so well mannered, solicitous and easy to be with that you can fall into the Libra love trap right away. Is it really a trap? Well, from the off you will find that Libra reserves the right to change their mind a dozen times before you even get together. The timing of the date is subject to alteration as Libra dithers and often something else comes up and they are caught in their own habitual dilemma about making decisions. You are expected to understand that none of this is their fault – you see, it can't be helped, they wouldn't want to upset anyone, so would you mind if it was all moved? Put like that, you are left feeling churlish that you do, in fact, mind!

Libra will, however, make sure that wherever you meet is a place that suits you. Indeed, they frequently prefer for the other person to choose the location. It takes the onus off them and means they are already off to a good start in terms of pleasing you, which they aim to do. However, if you take up these reins you run the risk of never really knowing what Libra likes and pretty soon they have fitted in around your own set-up. This is easy, but also it can be a little dull if you believe the whole point of a relationship is to have a significant other, not just a mirror reflection of your own wishes.

However, as Libra is actually more complex than they look, it is a mistake to assume that this 'perfect harmony' dating is a measure of what your relationship will be. Libra thrives on making continual adjustments – this is the function of the scales. Their contrariness will begin to make itself felt as you talk. One particular feature of Libra's engagement is that they will not necessarily take your side. As you regale them with your story of how unreasonable someone else has been, it can be quite unnerving to discover that Libra almost automatically takes the other person's point of view. They are not being disloyal or unsupportive – they simply need to see the other side of the argument and want you to see this too. You get the impression that life is seen in very rational terms and that anything you feel runs the risk of being deemed unreasonable in Libra's books.

The best aspect about dating a Libra is the sheer romance of it all. Libra believes in love, hearts and flowers and old-fashioned romance. They will do the honours in all forms and create an occasion. They will appreciate you and are never shy about giving compliments. So, you will be treated to a date that is designed to bring out the best in you, with the appropriate mood music (if you listen carefully you will hear the music of the spheres playing in perfect unison in the background!). Librans can be poetry in motion, no doubt about it.

Yet even in the dating stakes, there comes a time when you

might want to go a little deeper, venture out of the shallows to discover more about what makes your Libra really tick and who's inside that rather beautiful outer package. Occasional glimpses of their true heart essence are available, but going out of their depth frightens Libra and they shouldn't be forced or rushed. Therefore, conversational topics need to be kept light and non-threatening (even discussing your phobia of spiders could be seen by Libra as drawing them into a web!). It is all about 'having a nice time'. But then what? Despite the Libran desire for a relationship, their course rarely runs smoothly. They find themselves pitched into drama, or their own scales have tipped, so things are on and then off with alarming rapidity.

Very rarely will Libra accept responsibility for this state of affairs – it is far easier for them to claim not to know what happened or why, as if they are an innocent bystander rather than one half of the action. Libra believes in building people up and also letting them down very gently, so any shenanigans must be your fault!

As Libra is in love with love in a rather Disney-esque way it can be hard for them to deal with the detritus of human life, the reality of two human beings, complete with all their imperfections. Anything a little rough around the edges is anathema to this sign, so make sure you clean up well and put your best foot forward if you want to be part of the dating and mating, the somewhat stylised and ritualised courtship of Libra. Libra is not the sort that likes to get down and dirty. If you can exude the kind of grace and elegance Libra admires then love is the drug that will ensure they are hooked.

When all is said and done, Libra is on the pathway to self-discovery through relationships. They are on a lifelong mission to find out what compatibility really means. It is almost always not what they thought it was to start with. The balancing act that characterises a Libra in love requires them to compromise, negotiate and find the middle ground.

Dating your Libra love god or goddess requires you to have a pretty strong sense of self. To be the kind of person who can tolerate someone dancing around you without missing a beat. To know that most dances require the ability to step backwards as well as forwards. When Libra wants to be a partner, it is about the two of you and no one else. As you get to know each other well and thoughts might turn to a more permanent footing, then it's important to recognise that this is another line over which Libra must step. The question of commitment can trigger all manner of indecision, stalling, procrastination and U-turns. Treat it as a dance step and you'll still be together when the music stops.

Keeping . . . up Appearances
If you have managed to get Libra over the line and into a more permanent arrangement, an equal footing in terms of domestic arrangements and a union of hearts, then you are going to experience just how significant your 'other' can be. A wedding is a huge event for Libra, encapsulating as it does all the romance, public spectacle and entering into contract that makes Libra's world go round. They are the consummate wedding aficionado – loving every aspect of it. Whether it's the beach with the perfect sunset or the chapel with the most romantic arch of flowers, Libra will see to it that the event itself is the ultimate photogenic fantasy.

There are many more opportunities to fuel Libra's imagination when it comes to the perfect home, family and children. This sign can create photoshopped images of their lives in their heads without the aid of a smart phone or camera. The *appearance* of this union is important to Libra. That is not to say that they don't care if it's a dysfunctional nightmare underneath (Libra would become unbalanced with that), but they enjoy the output of a certain level of beauty and pleasantness. The premises, setting and personal appearance of this union must convey what Libra wants them to convey – that they have created and are living a beautiful life.

Harmony is a quality that Libra greatly admires. It is the glue that holds them together on the inside, so if your union is a constant diet of fireworks, the result is that Libra can literally go out with a bang. They will lose their own spark, withdraw and become increasingly frayed and miserable. Your Libran partner glows when they exist in an atmosphere of love and appreciation. They will do everything in their power to keep you happy, to maintain the partnership and are even capable of bending over backwards, almost contorting themselves, to accommodate your wishes.

Privately, your union with Libra is going to be the mainstay of life. You are each other's linchpin and if you are in love with your Libran, you will appreciate the feeling that the two of you are always better off together than apart. The real work of the relationship that begins after the fairy dust has settled is something that Libra has such a vested interest in. It is true that they do not want to be alone, but the fact is that they have chosen YOU! You will occupy the most central role in their universe – something that many other signs fail to acknowledge. Libra resonates with the feng shui belief that good luck is maintained in pairs.

Once you have lived with Libra long enough you get used to them being able to turn on a dime in an argument. The contradiction inherent in Libra's thinking requires you to polarise with them so you may at times find yourself forced into a particular position whilst they work out where they stand. Any thrashing out of plans has to be done with good nature as Libra seriously takes offence if you get into a slanging match. This sign can't stand rudeness and is not above completely annihilating your arguments whilst prefixing their intervention with 'can I ask you something please?' At other times you will feel as if you are in a tennis match against your other half as the plan gets lobbed back and forth between you until one of you serves an ace or drives it into the net.

Your union will grow stronger the more you play and if you form a doubles team then you really get to work with each other's strengths and challenges.

As Libra is a sign that begins with the autumn equinox – a time when day and night are of equal length – they are naturally predisposed to favouring equality. Libra sees marriage or partnership as a union of two halves, a striving for completeness through the harmonious joining of two sides. Perhaps more than any other sign they possess care and thought about the actual nature of partnership, what it really means. Of course when two families unite there are more people to consider and if Libra is also a parent, the mixing and matching and blending in order to form equality inevitably becomes more complicated, with Libra frequently complaining that they are caught in the middle of something. Their penchant for arbitrating between people can frazzle Libra!

In the bedroom, Libra is a romantic lover – no quick roll in last week's sheets for them. The whole experience is heightened by the most romantically evocative settings – Libra likes candles, high thread count and beauty all around. Yet it is not passion that Libra is after so much as the little touches to the heart. Passion can be too dangerous a place for them to inhabit for long and they prefer the bed of roses, the comfort of the marriage bed to the hurly burly of the chaise longue.

The Ex Factor: Going Halves
Doing the splits with Libra is never going to be straight forward as they dance the two step over the decision, sometimes for years. You see, Libra simply can't make up their mind what to do. They don't want to hurt you and they certainly don't want their precious dreams biting the dust – the tearing apart of all that was so beautiful and lovely, even if it plainly isn't now.

This is why Libra is capable of manoeuvring you into the position where you make the decision for them. In a passive-aggressive manner, they would prefer not to have to carry the can for the break-up. By making it your idea they feel they are absolved and can come out of it as the good person or even the wronged party – whatever they may have contributed to the relationship's demise.

Libra is, however, the kind of person to do the amicable divorce as they are repelled by outright hostility. Libran Gwyneth Paltrow is the champion of conscious uncoupling and has raised this idea to an art form, a gold standard of separation.

Division of assets is, of course, something that Libra will try to handle as fairly as possible. As they would any custody arrangements. In fact, your relationship will still exist in an important form long after you have ceased 'being together'. Libra doesn't just go off into the sunset without a backward glance – they will always have that little piece carved into their heart with your name on it.

DESTINY

The Libra Lovelies

As Libra is a people person they are the honeypot for bees. Yet for all Libra's diplomatic smiles, only the most appropriate or decorative will gain true entry to the tribe. Libra likes to move with the beautiful people or around the events of a gilded life. Even if this is just for high days and holidays. The kinds of people Libra likes to hang out with are refined, cultured and sophisticated. Their finely tuned sensitivity and aesthetic appreciation are unlikely to be met amongst a rowdy crowd and Libra will bow out of social arrangements that go against their grain (with a great deal of politeness, of course).

Libra's affinity with the divine feminine places both the men and women of this sign on the socially skilled, polite, graceful, artistically appreciative end of the scale. They work their charms on everyone within the group, perhaps not having a best friend for fear of offending someone, but being an enormously talented team player. They will always see both sides of any dispute but rarely commit themselves to total agreement with either. In fact, Libra can keep all the balls up in the air in any argument and have an astounding capacity to neutralise warring factions.

They are the person who is least likely to offend, the one who gets on with everyone, and this makes them essentially likeable and easy to be with. Yet there is something that remains distinctly unavailable about them. You can't draw them into contentious issues, or find out what drives them beneath the polished exterior. You can't share major upsets because they recoil in horror from all that shadowy stuff. Or, worse still, they sympathise with the enemy instead of condemning them as you might wish. Ah, it takes something extraordinary to get Libra down from the fence. They will be on your team but always reserve judgement just in case the other one is more deserving!

LIBRA

Ω

ALTAR OBJECTS

Place some of these objects on your altar or carry them with you in actual or pictorial form.

*

CRYSTAL: jade, topaz, aventurine, tourmaline

MINERAL/METAL: copper

LIBRA SYMBOLS: the scales, Venus

TAROT CARD: Justice

ANGEL CARDS: Angel Zuriel, Archangel Jophiel

FLOWERS: hydrangea, large daisy, bluebell

TREE: olive

SCENTS AND CANDLES: juniper, anise and violet

MEMORY BOARD/PHOTOGRAPHS/PICTURES: kisses, lips, romantic moments and places; painting: 'Venus and Cupid' by Lorenzo Lotto

CLOTH: fine silk in baby blue or pale aqua

TALISMAN: Venus, heart shapes

*

SCORPIO

SCORPIO

Treasures of the Underworld

♏

CORE QUALITIES: *intuitive, passionate, transforming power, intense*

Mantra: Today I will not give away my power.

The constellation of Scorpio: the brightest star in Scorpio is Antares. In the Northern Hemisphere, Scorpio lies close to the southern horizon. In the Southern Hemisphere, it lies high in the sky, close to the centre of the Milky Way.

Hold the gaze of a Scorpio and you will be taken somewhere . . . Most probably out of your comfort zone as that Scorpionic stare reaches into your soul, reading your Akashic records, penetrating your inner motivation and most certainly knowing everything about you that you would not put on Facebook.

There they are, these Scorpio creatures, often cool as a

cucumber, poised and still, but radiating out such intensity you are caught in an electromagnetic field that roots you to the spot. Even if you meet the bubblier type of Scorpio, do not be fooled – you are dealing with radioactive material. Scorpios know all about the mysterious, hidden aspects of human nature. Therefore, they see not only what you had for breakfast, but what you are thinking and what's more they understand why. It can be uncomfortable for those who prefer to carry on relationships in a 'normal' way. However, there is also something to be said for being seen and understood on a spiritual, cellular level. Scorpios possess insights and answers about human nature and life that you would never find on Google. This is a rare quality – and not to be underestimated.

Of course, Scorpio is famous for their sting. Yet it is true that most Scorpions would never lash out indiscriminately. It is simply not in their nature to lose control like that. It might be once in a lifetime, or never, or in answer to a particular hurtful experience, but it's not like you're going to get stung just for fun every day of the week. In fact, Scorpios are quite capable of stinging themselves if they feel they have crossed their own line, that they haven't upheld their own values. They will examine a situation and their own motives and feelings, turning everything over and over in their mind and if it is a case of mea culpa, they will punish themselves.

Scorpio searches for absolute truth. They are after all a sign of black and white rather than shades of grey and they hold strong opinions and principles. Ask a Scorpio what they think and you will be taken straight to the heart of the matter – their capacity to cut through all the fluff is astounding. This is again often uncomfortable for those who like to gloss over and cover up the cracks – Scorpio has no truck with that kind of behaviour and they deliver their piercing insights like an arrow of truth, rendering all your excuses and illusions null and void.

All Scorpios possess tremendous inner resourcefulness which may not be apparent to the naked eye. In fact, Scorpios like to stay low profile, fly under the radar. They do a great job of knowing all your secrets whilst you might have little idea of what's teeming underneath their poised exterior. In a crisis they can access huge reserves of power that enable them to rise again like a phoenix from the ashes. They emerge wiser and even more resilient and their life story can move in cycles of birth, death and rebirth almost as if they live several lives in one – this sign is the ultimate come-back king or queen.

Still waters run deep in Scorpio, they have access to unfathom-able depths in terms of life experience. This, complete with their psychic perception, can heal other people with their insights and presence and can effect transformation for anyone going through difficult times.

LIFE

Health

The great power of Scorpio's life force (*chi*) is emotionally super-charged energy that's waiting to be ignited in times of need.

They tend not to waste energy on inconsequentials but possess huge reserves when required. They are quite capable of defying doctors with their transformative, resurrective qualities and they are a sign that truly understands how it's possible to heal oneself.

Mind

Undoubtedly, Scorpio possesses huge mental capacity. They can train their penetrating mind on a subject and forensically focus on extracting every detail and meaning from it. Yet if they are not interested in something or someone it is as if that person or thing doesn't exist. Scorpio can totally ignore whatever they deem inessential.

As they cut to the chase, excavating the salient point, they often leave others wondering how on earth they got there so quickly. They have an unerring capacity to detect what lies beneath the surface – a Scorpio will never take anything at face value – so whilst others are distracted by appearances, Scorpio penetrates to the invisible material and produces it for others to see. It is often said about Scorpio that they have X-ray vision. This can, of course, come in useful, yet it's not always easy for Scorpio as they see what they may not necessarily want to see – other people's masks and facades come off and Scorpio sees the truth, no matter how unpalatable.

Body

Scorpio rules the reproductive organs – it is the sign associated with sexuality and birth. The male and female reproductive organs are the areas that contain the seeds of life – and they are normally hidden from view, in keeping with Scorpio's hidden power.

In terms of health, Scorpio is a sign that tends to repress a lot of emotion, yet feels things very deeply – and therefore they need to find a release for their passion and emotion or their energy turns stagnant.

Passion is their currency – sexual, mental and emotional – and if they don't have an outlet for passion then everything turns inward, creating a vast reservoir of unexpressed material which is not good for their health.

Spirit

The life path of Scorpio is usually complex and their journey takes them through dark and light places. Ultimately it is a path of renewal and revival, but few Scorpios get there without being tested by extreme emotional experiences. Interestingly, Scorpio considers an unexceptional smooth ride as exceedingly bland, preferring the ups and downs, the peaks and troughs as they recognise that negotiating these times only adds to their inner strength and makes them feel fully alive.

Spiritually and Karmically

The myth of Persephone, the innocent maiden being abducted into the underworld by Hades, is especially reflective of the spiritual journey of Scorpio. Certain things come up, the collision with unavoidable dark times that initiate Scorpio into some formidable tests for their soul, igniting their true power. This might involve betrayal or an element of fate and circumstance beyond their control – whatever it is, once Scorpio has been there and done that, they are up-levelled into a new frequency that at best gives them the capacity to offer unique insights into how to transform.

The ruling planet of Scorpio is Pluto – the celestial body now deemed by astronomers to be of reduced asteroid status rather than a planet, however anyone who has encountered Pluto's intractable power recognises that size is not an issue. His atomic properties do not relate to volume, but intensity of impact. All Scorpios brush with complex situations in their life – whether these are of their own making or seemingly a force of destiny. They learn to live with collateral damage, near obliteration in some situations – whatever has taken them to the edge of the abyss and back – and therein lies the tale of survival. A survival that can't be measured purely in physical terms, but can be a beautiful emotional renaissance too.

What Does Scorpio Have to Give?
Scorpio is the torchbearer for how to rebuild and start over, especially emotionally. Sometimes just knowing a role model who has managed this feat and vanquished tumultuous times is a precious gift, in terms of being able to imagine it is possible to 'have a new life'. But Scorpio will do better than that. They will actually help you get there yourself, offering all manner of guidance and practical assistance too if needs be. Scorpio is the person you turn to, no issue is too big, no crisis too appalling for them to proffer their calm and profound awareness of what you're going through and to help you heal from it.

Scorpio knows the wisdom of the ancient Chinese word for crisis, *wei-chi*, which matches crisis with opportunity. Inside every ordeal is a gift that will give you something worth having in life. Who better than Scorpio to assist you? The one who will leave no stone unturned when it comes to finding the gold in the darkest of matter. Scorpio is the alchemist who will accompany you through the processes of transformation and out the other side.

However, it's not just in a crisis that Scorpio are worth their weight in gold, but they know how to truly share themselves. The realm of intimacy is Scorpio's domain. They seek emotional as much as physical union, therefore you can feel extremely close to Scorpio as a friend, a co-worker – in fact, just having Scorpio in your book club gives you access to this preferential treatment. You will feel something is meaningful and significant about your connection with Scorpio, even if you rarely see them and you are talking about the weather. You just know they know! In other words – what is passed between you verbally is no measure of the depth of the connection you might feel because Scorpio can connect with you in ways that are hard to comprehend on an ordinary level.

What Does Scorpio Need to Receive?

Although Scorpio can wrest every last private anecdote and detail from you, perhaps making you feel a little exposed, it is a rare person who can put Scorpio so much at their ease that they will open up completely. Being able to ask the compelling and penetrating question that unlocks Scorpio's private quarters is an art – not many people can do it. But Scorpio will respect you for it and honour you with the VIP pass into their inner sanctum. As a sign full of secrets, both their own and other people's, Scorpio can feel relieved to unzip it a bit.

You can be sure that Scorpio has secrets – they are there in the Scorpionic aura, so you get the sense that there is always more to them than meets the eye. However, gaining their trust is no automatic entry. Sometimes, Scorpio can read you in such a way that their barriers come down instantly, they sense you are deep enough, loyal enough, sensitive enough to contain their private thoughts. Or it might take a while. They probe and hint but never fully reveal. With certain people, Scorpio will protect themselves to the nth degree, so much so that they seem entirely closed and a little stand-offish. Yet when Scorpio can truly trust it is a beautiful thing. If they can let their guard down, share with you, it brings out their more playful, engaging side.

When Scorpio lightens up it is as if the weather clears. In situations where you are relaxed, then Scorpio can be too. The more defensive you are, the more inclined to stick to shallow banter, then the greater the risk that Scorpio will freeze or glaze over. Engaging in a bit of deep-water diving followed by frolicking on the surface is the perfect scenario to get Scorpio at their very best.

What Does Scorpio Need to Learn?
It can be hard for Scorpio to accept that some people have no wish to or are terrified of engaging at the level on which Scorpio works. They might have no interest in transformation, personal development or the subjects that matter most to Scorpio. If Scorpio can live and let live, allowing everyone to be at their own level then they would suffer less rebuff from those who shrink away from the awareness that is Scorpio's lifeblood.

What about those grey areas, those places that lie in the middle that cause Scorpio to scratch their head and try to force towards a position at one end or the other? Scorpio needs to understand that there are even more than fifty shades of grey that are perfectly valid. Not everything has to be black or white. It is not that Scorpio is a totally rigid extremist, but they do need to loosen up a little when it comes to letting things be.

Forgiveness is another thing . . . Scorpio finds it hard to forgive, let alone forget when they have been wronged. Revenge may be a dish they feel is best eaten cold – but what about taking it off the menu altogether? As transcendence is another aspect of trans-formation, Scorpio at the highest level can get to rise above the bad. The eagle Scorpio can achieve this after a great deal of soul searching.

LOVE

Dating: Sirens and Seducers
Well, if you are dating a Scorpio you'd better know from the word go that this is going to be a passion – however long it lasts. You see, Scorpio isn't interested in bland, nice little relationships that tick along – they would rather have the full hurricane. You may never guess when you meet the full engagement of their eyes, whether it is across a crowded room or right in front of you, that you are about to enter a danger zone.

Dating Scorpio is not for the faint-hearted and certainly not for the fake or foolish. As Scorpio quickly becomes bored with shallow exchanges, you'd better have something profound, mysterious and deep about you. Besides, if Scorpio wants you in their life you have little choice in the matter, because their magnetic presence draws you to them. Some people feel as if a spell has been cast upon them. It isn't anything to do with the black arts, it is simply the Scorpionic sex appeal and silent sixth sense that compels you to go towards this person.

Often a Scorpio is unaware of the magnetic hold they can have on people, which is like an invisible lasso and often lasts long after the relationship is over. No one comes out of an encounter with Scorpio the same as when they went in. This is because Scorpio is the great transformer and your time spent with them will necessarily bring about greater awareness of yourself, life and the universe.

As Scorpio exudes great personal power it can be difficult to assess exactly where you might fit. Both men and women born under this sign give off a sense that they do not need anyone or anything – this is all part of their fear of needing something they cannot have. However, get close to Scorpio, gain their trust, and you will find they are so deeply soulful, in possession of such an intensely emotional nature coupled with that perceptive radar that you get up close and personal with what it means to be a Scorpio and understand how vulnerable they really feel. Which is why they cover it up. Get it?

There can be a sense of being reeled in – Scorpio is an acquired taste that can become addictive. If you are someone who needs a huge amount of personal space, who feels uncomfortable with intimacy and feelings then get out now. If you are happy swimming in the deep end, this could be one of the most meaningful relationships of your life. Certainly one that you won't forget and it will undoubtedly change who you are and how you perceive relationships from here on in.

For Scorpio, the best sort of relationship is meaningful and this runs the gamut from a kind of erotic/exotic quality to a transcendent union of souls, a mystical, mysterious connection that surpasses everyday human interaction. If you want to date a Scorpio it is best to reveal yourself in layers, to allow Scorpio to peel them off without flinching. They do see right through you, but they adore the intrigue of discovering what makes you tick slowly and deliciously. Little by little they will open up to you and you will receive depth-charged glimpses of the inner psychic battles they have fought and the insight it has brought.

Where to go and what to do with Scorpio is all about creating the right setting – the perfect backdrop to their nature. Think of private, perfectly intimate spaces that exude a slightly exotic or seductive aura. If you can't find that, then at least make sure you get the table that is tucked away so that Scorpio can be master of all they survey and feel protected from the fray.

Above all, when dating a Scorpio do not be taken in by their strong presence and assume that they are somewhat hard-bitten. You are dealing with a deeply sensitive person, no matter how well they hide it. They feel EVERYTHING – even if they give no reaction at the time. Remember, Scorpio is deceptively deep and sometimes rather unfathomable, like a great Scottish loch.

What of the trickier side of Scorpio's nature – their jealousy, possessiveness, their tendency to take the extreme viewpoint? It is best not to mess with Scorpio. If you are a player then steer clear; Scorpio requires the utmost loyalty. Their own life path might take them the circuitous route to discovering their moral integrity but Scorpios often walk on the dark side in order to get to the light. Yet once they have decided that you are really, truly worth their undivided love and attention then you will have their loyalty.

If you find Scorpio fascinating, then presumably you enjoy that spiritual kind of seduction that talks to your soul as well as your body. You may find that other people pale in comparison. Yes, they might be easier to be with on some level, but they will lack the capacity to give you that unique Scorpionic combination of steel and softness, of mystery and magnificence.

Scorpio will challenge you. You can't close off when they operate on a need-to-know basis and heaven help you if you have not been true on some level! In many ways, Scorpio wields a moral compass that is entirely of their own making and you are expected to conform to their ideals and integrity. However, Scorpio is like this because they know what happens when people betray other people. They may even have done so themselves and they understand the frailties of human nature, whilst at the same time holding to their own gold standard.

Between the sheets, Scorpio reveals more of themselves than ever before – and not just physically! This sign can smoulder and sizzle with seductive sexuality. They give out a passionate vibe that can be high or low volume but is always there. Scorpio believes intimate exchange is the major release, reviver, the major soul union between two people – that connects them forever across all lifetimes – and it will never be casual to them. Much has been made of Scorpio's somewhat obsessive nature which is born from their supernatural yearnings, cravings and wanting that is above and beyond what is considered by polite society to be normal. Scorpio has to constantly wrestle with their desires. If they want you then it can feel all-consuming and some will cross all kinds of thresholds in order to satisfy that want. Not much wonder they find it hard to control their complicated feelings and they also hate it that they want you so much because it means you have power over them – and anyone who has power over them might hurt them. So you are entering a dance of control and power, which carries alternating moves of intense passion followed by silence and withdrawal. This is so they can get a handle on their feelings. It can be make up/break up. It can be consuming passion followed by spiritual letting go. What it's not going to be is a normal trajectory. Scorpios blow hot and cold for a reason; it's not a game, it's just that their circuits blow and they need to cool off, calm down. Even in conversation they can share something so profound, intimate and intense and then go absent and inaccessible.

Dating is perhaps a term that doesn't even suit Scorpio. It smacks of something casual which isn't for them. Everything is meaningful for Scorpio, so your relationship must be too.

Otherwise it isn't worth their time or effort. Ultimately, Scorpio is looking for their soulmate and they will search and search across time and space until they find that electric spark, that mystical meeting that tells them this is the one.

Keeping . . . the Passion Alive
Once Scorpio has decided you are for keeps then you begin an entirely different kind of dance to the courtship ritual. Scorpions adore total intimacy – the kind that is 'they are yours and you are theirs and this is written in (metaphorical) blood'. It is almost like taking the initiation rites to a secret society (which it is!). Whilst other couples might be totally carried away in the romantic dream, Scorpio is on a different tack of the union of souls. It is not the cake and confetti, but the notion of karmic chords being tied that occupies them. Not that romance escapes them – after all, this is one of the most feeling signs on the planet and also one that rises to occasions, enjoying the dramatic intensity. A heartfelt exchange is what you will get with Scorpio, not someone caught up in pomp and ceremony.

Even if you don't make it a formal event and never sign on the dotted line, if Scorpio is your intended lifelong partner then you will enter into exactly the same karmic union in their books. As Scorpio doesn't do casual, making a relationship permanent is their idea of heaven. It takes away the uncertainty – although Scorpio will always wonder about betrayal as they know temptation is possible. They will always check you out to see where you've been and who you've seen – even if you've been together twenty-five years!

Don't think for one minute you will get one over on them,

unless you have a black belt in deception, as that psychic perception of theirs picks up clues and subtle alterations that most people would miss. They have an unerring instinct to 'just know' what's going on.

Let's be honest and say your Scorpio partner might not be the most easy-going person to live with (Scorpio always prefers honesty anyway). It's not that you won't have a lovely life, with an amazingly supportive partner, but you are expected to keep developing personally as no Scorpio can bear the static, rigid, 'I'm done with changing, learning, growing' kind of person around them. If your idea of long-term partnership is of slipping into inertia, then being with a Scorpio isn't for you. Yes, you can relax physically, but mentally, no! Scorpio wants to be on a permanent voyage of psychological discovery and stimulation.

The whole area of sharing what you have financially and emotionally is the Scorpio specialist subject. They are brilliant at growing resources, but there are some who are attracted by the destruction/creation cycle that lends itself to a scarier ride. Again this is the department where Scorpio has to find levels of trust that don't come naturally – along the way they experience issues to do with control. Sometimes it's just about who pays the bills, but it can be very deep-rooted and vested in legacies, properties and hidden bank accounts. Ultimately, Scorpio will learn lessons about the true value of people and money, and close relationships are often the trigger for their greatest learning.

Keeping the passion alive is another non-negotiable. This is because Scorpio feels almost dead without passion. Of course, they can find it in other spheres by pouring all that emotional intensity into mental pursuits, but then a part of them is locked up and it is as if someone has thrown away the key. As Scorpio is such a private person, if you are granted access to all areas then do not take it for granted.

The phrase 'behind closed doors' must have been invented for Scorpio because you get to see the Scorpionic drive, focus and inner resourcefulness close up. Scorpio channels their considerable power out into the world, but at home you see how it is created. Perhaps you feel you are living at Hogwarts! Your home will certainly be a place where the magic happens and it is the crucible of Scorpio's alchemy.

In private, of course there are going to be skirmishes – the Scorpio nature expects a lot, although they tend not to be overt about it like the Fire signs. You are simply required to give your best and, above all, to give a great deal of emotional attention to your Scorp, who will pour a huge amount of this into you too.

If there are troubles or any kind of crisis, then you have the perfect partner to sort them out. Scorpio will work through things, will exhibit a pure emotional strength that enables them (and you) to survive where other couples fall apart. The crisis can even make the partnership stronger as you will absolutely know the secret super-powers of your Scorpio.

And you just have to admit there is no one else who could have turned things around quite like Scorpio. You will never know if it's totally over with Scorpio until it's totally over! Even then . . . never say never.

Ex Factor: Exit, Extraction, Expired

This can be troubled territory, depending on how your relationship broke up. If you have betrayed Scorpio then you are likely to experience the full volcanic eruption. Not a pretty sight and a veritable minefield. However, what did you expect? If you have broken the trust of a Scorpio then in their opinion you have committed a very deep crime and hurt them so badly that all the intense love they gave you turns to fear, hurt and backlash. They are hardly going to say, that's absolutely fine darling, just shatter my heart and everything's OK.

You will see Scorpio go through all the stages of grief, anger and final acceptance – and this could take years. Scorpio will eventually get to the peaceful dove in their nature or the magnificent phoenix that rises again. However, if your Scorpio is the person who takes off then it is likely they will want to remain friends with you and retain a unique and very special relationship. You can come to Scorpio years after your relationship has technically broken down and they will still totally get you.

When children are involved, Scorpios make them their number one priority. As a parent, Scorpio usually fiercely protects their offspring and can be a positive role model in terms of handling difficulties.

Financially and emotionally, once Scorpio gets back on their feet – and they always will, even if they go through a bleak period – you will see how amazingly resilient they are. They are perfectly capable of having a new life which bears no resemblance to the old one, as if reincarnation happens in this lifetime.

DESTINY

Tribal Dance

Scorpio is not a team player who necessarily wants to play *your* game. Once you get into that scenario with Scorpio you will discover they will outwit you at every turn or simply not want to play. They are great at finding the right people, seeing people's strengths and weaknesses, and putting them together.

In friendship, Scorpio is the most loyal you will ever find. The opposite of the fair-weather friend, Scorpio is totally there for you when things get tough. They're absolutely stalwart in terms of helping you get through problems and particularly brilliant at helping you understand why something happened and what can be done so you get the perspective to move on.

With Scorpio you will be privy to their deepest secrets if they trust you enough. There is a grading system in operation and if they don't open up, then chances are you're not in the top tier. However, they will still offer you their full depth of understanding if you are the one who needs it.

However, cross a Scorpio – especially in front of other people – and you will exact retribution. Scorpio can go as far as acting like you are dead to them. Because they are inherently loyal to you they are gutted by disloyalty shown to them and find it very hard to take you back into the fold. Even if they go through the motions of friendship and pleasantries you will be personally frozen out of any kind of important exchange.

Scorpios love to share experiences that are truly meaningful and rich in feeling. Purely superficial friendship doesn't even exist for them. If you are in their life, then you have been hand-picked and selected for your own exceptional qualities. To know a Scorpio and work and play with them is an honour you will feel grateful for. They give you a lot, both visibly and invisibly; just being in their presence ups your EQ and your game beyond measure.

SCORPIO

♏

ALTAR OBJECTS

Place some of these objects on your altar or carry them with you in actual or pictorial form.

*

CRYSTAL: amethyst, topaz, obsidian

MINERAL/METAL: steel

SCORPIO SYMBOLS: the scorpion, eagle, dove

TAROT CARDS: The High Priestess, Wheel of Fortune

ANGEL CARDS: Angel Barbiel, Archangel Jeremiel

FLOWERS: geranium, rhododendron, orchid

TREE: chestnut

SCENTS AND CANDLES: iris, orange blossom, coriander, amber, patchouli

MEMORY BOARD/PHOTOGRAPHS/PICTURES: powerful images of people or events, ancestors; painting: 'Persephone' by Dante Gabriel Rossetti.

CLOTH: velvet in ruby red

TALISMAN: scorpion, jewel-coloured charms

*

SAGITTARIUS

SAGITTARIUS

Bring Me My Arrows of Desire

CORE QUALITIES: *adventurous, playful, optimistic, excessive, tactless*

Mantra: Today, I enjoy living in the moment without fast-forwarding into the future.

The constellation of Sagittarius: Sagittarius was one of the forty-eight constellations listed by Ptolemy, an astronomer in the 2nd century AD. Sagittarius is at the centre of the Milky Way.

The archer is always on a mission, the more impossible the better, because for them, everything is always possible. Their glass-half-full mentality means that there are no limits to what the future holds. They are usually so positive that the universe listens to what they say and gives it to them – a form of the law of attraction. It's all good. Except when it isn't, and the archer fires off arrows using people as targets until his temper burns out. Usually, it doesn't last long but it's important to remember that this go-getting sign of the zodiac is a force of nature. Sagittarius is also known as the centaur – half man, half horse – and therefore you are dealing with a strange creature, moving between the higher and lower self, the elevated quest and the base instincts.

Sagittarius is always fun to be around and is adept at living life large, pushing the edges and boundaries further and further to see just how far they will go. They love to feel life is opening up and expanding, that they are onto something – whether it's discovering a greater meaning or a new place to eat. It really doesn't matter which, as long as it's a new horizon.

The truth about Sagittarius is that they have a huge appetite for life. They also want to have a really good time here on planet Earth. This can mean a lot of hedonistic and party-animal behaviour, especially when young, but could evolve into a wisdom about life gained from the far corners of the world (they are inveterate globetrotters) and picking up nuggets of truth from all their encounters.

Sagittarius doesn't do well stuck in a box, in an office or in stationary traffic. They must *move* and the minute they feel limitation, the impatience of their fire-sign nature comes to the fore. They can literally gallop off with barely a backward glance. Their eyes are always trained on the future and so they are much more interested in tomorrow rather than today. Whilst some signs are hemmed in by their attachment to the past, Sagittarius fast forwards into the future. It is all about possibility, potential and what might unfold. Even if they don't hit the bullseye, the archer enjoys the process of firing arrows at the target. They can spot where things might lead and they take their chances rather than the safe option.

The archer is the searcher – whether they are looking for fun and adventure or greater meaning. Their joy is in the quest to find something and it is the journey rather than the destination that grabs them. In fact, having arrived, all they can think of is where to go or what to do next. Standing still and savouring the moment is a major difficulty for them! It's all about what's out there and their infectious enthusiasm can inspire other people to do things they may not have had the courage for before. Of course, they can get carried away, overlooking risks that would loom large in other people's perceptions. However, Sagittarius is usually able to come up trumps. They have a real gift for making the best of most situations.

Then there is their sense of humour. They have a capacity to laugh at just about anything. Perhaps they have more of a problem taking life seriously than other people. But don't forget they have that wise streak and being able to laugh at misfortune is a great advantage.

LIFE

Health

The Sagittarian tendency to not know when to stop can create imbalance. They have to find their own off button or they just keep going, eating, drinking, partying, staying up, overdoing it. Tuning in to the limits of the body rather than pushing everything too far is their great lesson. The archer is ruled by Jupiter – planet of abundance and indulgence – and guess which organ of the body it takes its toll on? The liver is the main organ associated with Sagittarius.

Mind

Sagittarius is a sign of vision. They are the 'big picture' people, seeing the overall trajectory rather than bothering with the details. In keeping with their element, they tend to start ideas like fires but leave them to others to tend, quickly getting bored and moving on.

Perhaps their most frequent question is, 'What is the point of this?' because unless they can see where something might lead they lose interest. It is hard for them to dwell on things purely for their own sake. They can learn a vast amount, accrue a whole body of knowledge, clock up miles of travelling if it interests them. But expect them to go over something they've already done and you'll see that Sagittarius just can't get excited enough to apply themselves.

They can grasp huge concepts, sell ice to Eskimos, but the everyday boring bits are not their bag. Sagittarius needs to employ their mental energy in motivating themselves and others.

Body

In keeping with their journey of growth, Sagittarians are often tall, impressive looking and sporty but, of course, you get the slighter types that still exude a huge amount of excess energy as if they are irrepressible (which they are). The liver is the organ that has to deal with processing everything that the body ingests. If Sagittarius lives in excess then the liver really needs to detox. On a more spiritual, energetic level the liver is also responsible for processing feelings, and a sluggish or stagnant liver is one that is overwhelmed with and bombarded by too much of everything.

Sagittarians are active, fiery types and need to burn off excess energy. Hips and thighs are another area associated with this sign – mobility being important for these areas. They have a huge need to be doing things and they enjoy physical challenges. Wide open spaces and nature appeals to them. They are the ramblers, hikers, cross-country joggers. The rawness and beauty of nature matches their frequency and they often feel a huge affinity with wildlife and animals.

Spirit

Sagittarians possess a strong and generous spirit that is open to people, life and all experiences. Their wide-eyed friendliness makes their world larger and their interest in other cultures means they can connect with anyone. Being positive and warm enables them to create their own luck. Sagittarians usually believe everything that happens is for the best, that it is meant to be and they take any setback with astounding good humour.

Spiritually and Karmically

Being ruled by the planet Jupiter which is associated with Zeus, it's little wonder that most Sagittarians can identify with being a sky god. Nothing less will do! Zeus, the champion of Mount Olympus, ruled with thunderbolts and lucky strikes – forever chasing, zooming hither and thither and pretty much unassailable. Most Sagittarians have an innate sense that they are here on planet Earth to either have a really good time, make a really big difference or to help teach others a bit about the meaning of life. Usually all three are rolled into a single incarnation!

What Does Sagittarius Have to Give?

As chief cheerleader, Sagittarius is usually able to encourage others to look on the bright side or to look at lessons learned in any experience as a gift. In one way, the archer can take people out of ruminating, dwelling and blaming by the sheer vital force of their personality, their belief that all will be well. It's hard to be negative in the face of their positivity – unless you get a kick out of polarising with people. So, knowingly or not, Sagittarius can lift you out of yourself, take you to a higher level of perception and create a much broader context in which to view any problem you might have.

Sagittarius is all about growth and development. Their curiosity about what things might become means that absolutely everything is an 'opener'. They see possibilities that pass others by. They might see some that don't exist or won't come to pass, but their position on a never-ending conveyor belt of opportunity is certainly food for thought.

Being essentially good-natured and good-humoured is also conducive to bringing out the best in others. Being able to see the funny side can be quite a gift when laughter becomes the best medicine. Sagittarians are never stingy about sharing themselves, freely giving their warmth and enthusiasm which is like walking Prozac for some folk. Then there is their unerring ability to create fun, largely to do with their expectation and intention of having the good times roll, which in turn tends to result in a better time to be had by all.

What Does Sagittarius Need to Receive?

When archers lose focus and employ the scatter-gun technique, they need a steadying hand, a voice of reason to pull them back when they get carried away. As a counter-balance, Sagittarius needs to be with people who have their feet planted firmly on the ground, those who dare to tell them about the practical pitfalls of taking great risks. Sagittarians might be born under a lucky star – and there is a saying that fortune favours the brave – yet pushing their luck can trip them up. If you can be a sounding board for some of their outlandish propositions, you might even find Sagittarius listens instead of leaping in.

Being in the present is difficult for those born under this sign. Accepting things as they are is not their forte because they want to know where it's all going to lead or what they could do to improve the situation. If you are the kind of person who has staying power, you can astound Sagittarius with a lesson learned. It may even stop them looking over your shoulder to see who else is walking into the room (which is symbolic of their entire attitude to life). Captivating their attention is no mean feat.

Generous by nature, the archer can be cast in a role as the giver of favours. Taken to extremes, they can feel like a purveyor of freebies so it is a wonderful thing to watch Sagittarius actually receive something, to be given to. It's not that they really need anything – the archer will shrug things off, make light of any problems they might have – but it is a light-bulb moment for them to discover that someone else can facilitate making things happen for them.

What Does Sagittarius Need to Learn?

As the Sagittarian vision is large-screen, they miss the details. It is all about moving along instead of being in the moment. The archer also has a reputation for being careless, for riding rough-shod over the finer points in their quest towards getting where they want to go. Broad, sweeping gestures sometimes fail to take in the starker reality as Sagittarius looks towards the pot of gold rather than acknowledging the actual hard work entailed in achieving it. Some Sagittarians simply never grow up or find the capacity to stick at anything.

Being honest is what they call their famously blunt delivery. Words tumble out as they speak as they see. They can be indiscreet and careless about your sensitivities, laughing them off as if they shouldn't really matter. If they do, then you are left feeling as if someone has trampled all over you.

Sagittarians need to learn to turn down the volume, to be still – this is where their true philosophical wisdom resides, their inner self. Moving from external to internal is the real journey of Sagittarius, no matter how many miles they cover in life, no matter what adventures they clock up.

LOVE

Dating: Firing those Arrows of Desire

The romance of chasing after someone they desire is such a thrill for the archer. But beware, the clue is that the romance is in the chase rather than the capture. If you are being pursued by an archer, best to keep moving. Seriously, make it too easy and Sagittarius will quickly lose interest. As this sign is attracted to potential, you would do well to remain a possible rather than a probable for as long as you can!

Similarly, if you wish to date an archer then don't imagine that going to the local pub is going to be enough to hold them, unless you've got great tales of exploration to keep them fascinated. To make an archer happy you've got to inspire them, tease them, make them laugh, tell them something they don't already know and preferably go somewhere with them that opens up new horizons – whether it's Namibia, an all-night comedy club or trying out a triathlon.

Archers wear their hearts on their sleeves; the warmth of the Fire sign is infectious and they are so easy to get along with that you feel you are instantly compatible, even if you are not! They cover a broad range of subjects, experiences and people and you can take them to any party and they will be the life and soul. Hedonistic, party-animal Sagittarius will certainly want those good times to roll. Having fun is very important to them – it's all about high days and holidays. Archers can either give an impression of being on a permanent gap year, or if they hold down a 'sensible' job, mitigate the seriousness of it by making up for lost time in the evenings and on weekends.

It's hard to get them pinned down for a date when their diaries are already full – but Sagittarius is a spontaneous creature and will hastily rearrange what was planned if something better comes along. They are almost always 'up for it' if you suggest taking off for something at the last minute. But it has to be really appealing and give them that adrenaline rush, that excitement of adventure.

Sitting still for long is not their idea of a good time so keep them on the move, throw other people into the mix and don't go big on intimacy or you run the risk of scaring them away. If you can stand casual dating then this sign is great! You might find yourself in rotation with other 'possibles' as archers usually know a lot of people who may or may not be more than 'just good friends'. They won't lie to you about it, their honesty precludes that. In fact, you might find yourself wishing they didn't always give you 'too much information'. But playful as they are, Sagittarians are not players in the love stakes. They have too big a love of life to spend their entire time juggling people's hearts. They are generally straightforward and if you are energetic enough to keep up with them then you will find their arrow of desire has hit you right on target.

So if you have got past the initial stage, become more than a casual fling and successfully negotiated the first date, the first kiss and moved onto hanging out together then you may be able to relax a little more as clearly your archer finds you very interesting and worth exploring. Your relationship might feel more like buddies than boyfriend/girlfriend due to this sign's inherent dislike of the concept of couple-dom. If you can cope with that and realise that friendship underpins everything else then you're onto a winner.

Archers are one of the most positive signs of the zodiac but they don't like to attract the opposite in terms of a negative outlook. Being playful with your archer is sure to keep them engaged. The relationship is likely to progress quite fast if they like you, as archers are quick, bold and active. They won't hold back out of shyness or reserve. In fact, they are very direct and have a 'let's get on with it' mentality.

If you are the kind of person who takes hours to get ready, who observes formalities and 'the rules' of dating, then this is unlikely to be a match made in heaven. Sagittarius likes to make things up as they go along, they want the relationship to develop and unfold without preconceptions and expectations. They also prefer you au naturel than perfectly put together. Relaxation is key for Sagittarius and the more controlled you are about looks and appearance, the less appeal you hold for them.

If you're looking for someone to make you laugh, bring out the best in you, be a positive, life-enhancing influence then Sagittarius is the one. In return you should offer up a challenge, be capable of playing like puppies and not be the kind to throw tantrums or be especially needy. In fact, Sagittarius is a 'no worries' kind of person. Using the relationship as a container or punchbag for emotional problems is not going to fit with their need for freedom and fun.

Archers may not be the most emotionally intimate or physically tender sign of the zodiac. In fact, some Sagittarians treat getting close as a kind of sport. They are athletic, outdoorsy and can bounce around like Tigger, so don't expect roses and romantic seduction. It is more likely to be kisses around the barbeque or campfire.

Commitment phobia is sometimes an issue for Sagittarius who prefers life to be light and carefree. They have a fear of being trapped, suffocated or settling into the horrors of domesticity. They don't want to waste a second of their precious fire-sign life dealing with blocked drains, emotional dramas or weeding the window boxes!

Of course, there are the Sagittarians who hold you in thrall with their mental questing, their astounding knowledge of the night sky, of the *Iliad*, the mating habits of the leatherback turtles and the mysteries of Atlantis. They will certainly keep your brain on its toes! In keeping with their search for advancement, Sagittarians never stop learning and that makes them enormously stimulating and interesting!

Keeping . . . the Home Fires Burning
If you've managed to persuade your centaur that home is where the heart is – or the hearth for that matter – and you want to keep that flame alive then you must recognise the truth of the saying: 'If you want to keep something set it free'. This is essential in order to keep your archer coming back to you. They are the original hunter-gatherer types and have absolutely no wish to be at home tending the fire, but they can hold a torch for you forever if you give them space to do so.

When it comes to nuptials and formal occasions, archers like to keep things relatively fuss-free. They can handle the spiritual aspect of tying the knot, the party and the after party, but expect them to get excited about seating plans and speeches and you'll see how wild horses are not made for the altar. The whole idea of you two being together as far as Sagittarius is concerned is all about setting off on the journey of life together. If there is real travel involved then so much the better. Besides, archers get antsy focusing on just one day when there are so many days stretching out ahead. They get impatient and restless and if you're not careful they might wish it would soon be over.

If you're not going down that route and have decided to go barefoot on the beach, or to ignore having a wedding ceremony altogether, then you will have let yourself off the very hook that irks Sagittarius about the idea of getting hitched. The archer is absolutely capable of loving you forever without the need for any witnesses or piece of paper. The sense of choosing to be with you delights this sign and perpetually feeling that choice is theirs to make over and over again is a personal freedom they enjoy.

Going the distance with Sagittarius is all about 'the future', which beckons like a glittering array of opportunities and possibilities. Sag adores the feeling that you have enriched their life instead of 'tied them down'. Opening up, adding on, enhancing, is much more preferable than feeling they are going to miss out on the freedom of the single life. With Sagittarius as a partner it is best to have a sense of purpose together, that you're going to do things, create a life, experience wonderful adventures. Having something to look forward to will always be paramount.

In terms of domestic arrangements, the archer is not the most tidy creature on Earth. Slapdash, always in a rush, throwing things together . . . Don't expect a domestic god or goddess. They like space around them, room to move about and the kind of home where people are welcome to drop in at any time. Open house is their natural way of being, the more the merrier as it helps offset their fear of suffocation. They are often out and about and doing things – anything that engages them with the world instead of sitting at home.

Surprising your archer is a great way to keep the playfulness alive – routine is anathema to them. If it sounds as if this half horse/half human is hard to tame, well you'd be right. However, wasn't it precisely that wild streak that attracted you to them in the first place? You need to think of your union as being made of very strong elastic that will stretch without breaking.

If you have got yourself an archer who has already learned that too much of a good thing can be detrimental, you can thank your lucky stars. This is the more evolved type of Sagittarian who has lived life in the fast lane and moved over. They have learned how to put the brakes on which makes for a smoother relationship!

Sagittarius can be a little clumsy, goofy, seem as if they are not taking life seriously. But don't underestimate the sage that lies within. Just when you think you've reached the end of your tether, your archer will come out with something so profound and wise that you wonder where it came from. In a single sentence they can say something that vanquishes all your fears, stresses and problems and alters your whole angle of perception. They have this gift of being able to download knowledge directly from their higher self, their evolved wise person within.

And there you have it, your very own sage/centaur right on your doorstep! Who needs a guru when your life partner can suddenly turn into an ascended master?

As a Fire sign, although undoubtedly the most good-humoured of the lot, don't forget that Sagittarius will have flashes of temper as their patron Zeus, god of thunderbolts will make appearances from time to time. However, laughter solves and soothes most things for the archer. They might get heated but it is quickly forgotten – that is one of the pluses of the Sagittarian ability to move on.

Keep growing as a couple and you will experience incredible vistas that open up as the years go by. Sagittarius is a fun parent, adoring involvement in sports and education and any excuse to be playful.

There's a lot to be said for having such a positive partner. Someone who will make you smile, who will challenge you, make life fun and never feel they are too old to do anything, whether it's climbing Machu Picchu or flying a kite.

The Ex Factor: Burned Out
If your time with the archer has run its course then usually there are no grudges. That is, unless your half-horse has bolted, leaving you aghast and with a pile of consequences to clear up. You see, Sagittarius doesn't do consequences. They live in the future, not the past – so when something is over, it's over and they gallop away to pastures new. It can be hurtful to realise you were just an experience and they have moved on quickly. Yet on the other hand they are very keen to remain friends and to have the best possible outcome for this separation.

If you are the one closing the curtains on this relationship then your Sagittarian will be bewildered because they may not have picked up on your clues that things were not right. Being relent-lessly optimistic they don't want to chew over problems and sometimes find them hard to acknowledge – so they are not the type to spot trouble in the air.

You might feel that your archer has been careless with you – you didn't get the reassurance and love you were looking for. That's because Sagittarius believes actions speak louder than words and their presence in your partnership spoke volumes.

The Sagittarius parent likes to be the 'fun' parent, which can be hard for those left with all the responsibilities. However, they want to keep things amicable between you and to make the most of the situation.

Perhaps you too should put your time with the archer down to being an amazing learning curve. You have to admit that this person expanded your horizons and opened up a new perspective for you.

DESTINY

The Tribe – Gang Culture

The archer loves people. They like nothing better than entering into team challenges, sporting or otherwise, and experiencing adventures with friends and co-workers. They are so global that their tribe is gathered from all corners of the world. There are no barriers, no limitations. Sagittarius is a brilliant team motivator and so enthusiastic and inspiring that the team spirit is lifted. Their motto is 'there is nothing we can't achieve together'.

So if you want to be part of a fun time, if you can keep up with the fast pace and are up for the challenge, then being part of the archer's gang is a wonderful experience. Party poopers are not accepted. High-maintenance friendships that involve long emotional monologues are put on the back burner. The fire of Sagittarius wants to burn bright, to make things happen.

Of course, staying power is not their thing so you have to take your chances and realise that Sagittarius will not want to repeat what you did last time you got together; they will want to look for the next adventure. Life will never be dull around them – keep your passport, dancing shoes and Fitbit at the ready!

SAGITTARIUS

↗
✕

ALTAR OBJECTS

Place some of these objects on your altar or carry them with you in actual or pictorial form.

*

CRYSTAL: lapis, turquoise, ruby

MINERAL/METAL: tin

SAGITTARIUS SYMBOLS: the archer, the centaur

TAROT CARD: Temperance

ANGEL CARDS: Angel Adnachiel, Archangel Raguel

FLOWERS: lilac, amaryllis, gladioli

TREE: fig, mulberry

SCENTS AND CANDLES: sandalwood, cardamom, ginger, water lily

MEMORY BOARD/PHOTOGRAPHS/PICTURES: globe, wild horses, travel pictures, party invitations; painting: 'Deianeira and the Centaur Nessus' by Guido Reni

CLOTH: felt in orange or light blue

TALISMAN: Jupiter, lucky coin

*

CAPRICORN

CAPRICORN

Cautious Climber

♑

CORE QUALITIES: *solid, controlled, purposeful, self-reliant, serious*

Mantra: I relax with every cell of my being.

The constellation of Capricorn: Capricorn is a faint constellation with only one star above magnitude +3. It was first catalogued by Ptolemy in the 2nd century AD.

The mountain goat tenaciously and sure-footedly climbs his path up the mountain. This symbolic mountain represents a pinnacle of desired achievement, which is different for each and every Capricorn. Yes, there are many for whom worldly success, recognition and material goods are seen as the height of ambition. Yet Capricorn can also tread a path of spiritual evolution that is equally challenging and their end game might be to achieve a blend of material and spiritual reward.

Being tested is a Capricorn 'thing'. Partly because this sign believes in the core of their being that anything worth having must be earned. They tend to mistrust what lands in their lap, feeling that they haven't worked for it and therefore are non-deserving. Capricorn is serious about life. They have a sense of purpose that drives them on; even when others have given up, the mountain goat will carry on surviving and thriving.

This sign has a mature outlook and as children tend to be wise beyond their years, a little shy and contained. It is only much later in life that Capricorn will relax. As Saturn (Chronos) is their planetary ruler they have an in-built timing mechanism that apportions their life experiences so that they hold something in reserve for later.

Naturally ambitious, Capricorn always keeps an eye on where they are heading and very rarely strays off that path. They can be single-minded, a little uptight or even repressed when it comes to emotional expression. Their strength lies in self-containment so they hold their feelings in and can seem quite defensive, closed down and well protected. Yet their grip on reality is so impressive that they can take on huge responsibilities and, having managed them successfully, self-worth follows.

When it comes to self-discipline, Capricorn is the person who wears the hair shirt, who is capable of denying themselves pleasure. But they are of the Earth element and therefore hardly immune to all the luscious, sensual pleasures of life. It's just that they know when and how to rein it in a bit.

Security is what they long for – and Capricorn devotes great tracts of their time to establishing it, preferably in tangible form. They are no fly-by-night, flaky types. They are slow-burners, the steady and stable ones.

LIFE

Health

Capricorn has what's known as a strong constitution. They can endure the impact of life on the physical plane with a certain hardiness. Their sign is associated with the skeletal system and skin. So bones, the back, teeth and joints can show wear and tear and nervous ailments can show on their skin. Generally, this sign knows how to take care of themselves and can develop a routine that keeps them in good working order. However, as health is not purely about the body but stems from the relationship between mind, body and spirit they often fail to appreciate that repressing their feelings will eventually show up in physical form.

Mind

Although this sign is renowned for practical thinking, rooted in reality, they are also in touch with a more spiritual perspective – those mountain peaks provide inspiration from above. However, a Capricorn will never jump to conclusions or go off on tangents. They follow a pragmatic path and are not given to wild flights of fancy. This is why others turn to Capricorn for their reality check and quite simply this sign will bring people down to earth. However, they can be pessimistic, looking on the downside, focusing on the flaws rather than the possibilities. Capricorns can get stuck in a negative outlook, perhaps as a defence against disappointment – yet, of course, being negative tends to attract experiences that confirm those thoughts.

This sign is brilliant at planning, organising and managing. They can put something together which is built to last and tend to have a good business brain. What they lack in spontaneity is more than made up for in terms of longevity. The tortoise wins the race.

Body

The naturally conservative Capricorn is almost always well put together and poised. They possess great staying power in their physical nature. In fact, their stamina is incredible. Capricorn is still standing, cool, calm and collected when other signs have long since keeled over. Very good at pacing themselves, Capricorn is innately sensible about how to treat the physical body, how to live within the confines of the body, and their capacity for self-discipline is often applied to diet and exercise with great results.

Their energy is measured, contained and controlled. Poised and polished, this is the sign that respects life on the physical plane and works hard to maintain it. Many Capricorns look years younger than their age, even though as children they seemed so much older than their peer group because of their maturity. Flexibility is the quality they need to develop – to keep themselves moving and flowing and to recognise that freezing their feelings is a precursor to the body getting stuck too. Interestingly, they are often attracted to mountains – climbing, skiing, hiking – they are magnetically drawn to those peaks.

Spirit

It may not seem obvious that Capricorn's strive to climb uphill in the world, seemingly doing battle with practical obstacles, is, in fact, a spiritual rather than a material struggle. Yet, in surmounting great difficulties, this sign actually purifies their spirit, developing resilience, humility and endurance. Saturn is associated with reward for effort – and Capricorn delays gratification, believing that they should do the right thing both for themselves and others.

Spiritually and Karmically

Karma is a concept that belongs to the domain of Saturn and rather neatly fits with the Capricorn view that what you put in is what you get back. However, sometimes Saturn requires them to graduate from the school of hard knocks and lessons learned, which this sign tends to take on the chin, dutifully dealing with all that comes their way. That is not to say that the life of a Capricorn is relentlessly gritty – rather that they do not waste time on inessentials and are pragmatic enough to realise that proving themselves is an honest way forward.

It's almost as if Capricorn incarnates with a sense of duty – that they are here for a purpose and must keep sight of it. They have no desire to lose their footing on the slippery slope, but to ascend.

What Does Capricorn Have to Give?

Capricorn is an Earth sign – solid, durable and built to last. It is the most stalwart of signs. That might not sound glamorous but it is such a valuable quality and still there when the more ephemeral and sparkly bits have fallen off other signs. Capricorn possesses the loyalty and persistence that lasts forever. Their sound common sense, professionalism and mature outlook is well loved in the business community but should be appreciated everywhere as being of intrinsic value and the perfect antidote to the more vacuous, shallow components of modern culture.

There is the saying that if you want to get something done, ask a busy person. It could be tweaked slightly to be 'ask a Capricorn' as this sign will always do their best to support, help, achieve and complete. They're not the type to make fake promises, to give up or fail you. Something in them feels morally bound to give their best to life in general and to you, if you ask.

This sign is great at holding things together through thick and thin. Very few possess their internal resilience and capacity for hard work. Their commitment to the end result is an inspiration.

What Does Capricorn Need to Receive?
The mountain goat is so straight, so buttoned up, that you can easily think their work is never done. Yet they long to be released from their own emotional straight jacket. It's a great joy to see Capricorn loosen up, find their pleasure and finally relax. They can do so in the company of those they love and trust. It's almost as if their suit of armour is for the outside world. Once you spot the chinks in it and can persuade them to take the whole thing off, then you will see the real earthy Capricorn underneath, delighting in humour (theirs is bone dry) and with the capacity to enjoy and take their pleasures as seriously as their work.

Of course, they sometimes need to be reminded to stop being so serious. Their anxiety is about being respected – almost as if they are so vulnerable that their self-image would crumble if they let their guard down. Yet once they feel safe with you, you'll see that Capricorn can become lively – indeed, really good company.

It does them good to be around those who are less self-conscious, those who can ruffle the mountain-goat hair and enable them to relax.

At times Capricorn can be perceived as somewhat cold or even calculating. They are not ones to wear their heart on their sleeve. But again, this is usually because they fear their own vulnerability and build walls to keep them safe. If you can be the one who takes down a few bricks by exuding the kind of warmth and emotional engagement that reaches through barriers, then you will be surprised at how they open up to you.

What Does Capricorn Need to Learn?
As this sign tends to become engrossed in their own trajectory it's hard for them to step outside of their own structured thinking, to allow outside interference. Contained and controlled Capricorn can miss out on a lot simply by never daring to experience something that might be a risk, or outside of their own carefully maintained comfort zone.

Trust is the big one for those born under this sign. They sometimes seem as if they are permanently waiting for the other shoe to drop – and calling that realistic! Yet they tend to ripen late and as they get older, this sign can drop their reserve more easily.

In keeping with the scaling of heights, Capricorn tends to have a rather hierarchical view of life. They are super aware of levels, status, recognition, honours, credentials, reputation and exclusion zones. Yet in defining themselves and others by these classifications, life can become rather limiting and one of Capricorn's life lessons is to develop a more open-door policy and to take people for who they are. Material reality is always going to be very important to them, but gaining knowledge of the emotional energies and more subtle exchanges between people is a revelation. Learning not to keep everything inside but to share freely and spontaneously is a road to greater happiness. Perhaps Capricorn retains a certain cynicism, yet a more healthy approach is not to make judgements in advance but to go in with an open mind and heart.

LOVE

Dating: in the Slow Lane

One thing you need to know for sure when dating a Capricorn is that this thing will not take off like a rocket. For that, try a Fire sign, but you are currently with a mountain goat, who is naturally shy, inherently cautious and steady. Capricorn won't even ask you out unless they have undertaken a vetting process, checked you out, Googled you, watched you and decided that you are a deserving recipient of their time and energy. That might sound stand-offish or high-handed, but you see, this sign simply doesn't want to be around someone who isn't the right type for them.

What is their type? Well, they might think that they are looking for the person who will augment their own climb to the top. Undoubtedly, some Capricorns are very impressed by those who possess the talents or status that will keep them on the road to advancement. But not all Capricorns are that kind of climber. There are those who are looking for something serious, long term and committed – a relationship that will be stable rather than just a few dates. It helps too if you can offer that bridge for Capricorn to cross, from the practical and material to the emotional or creative side of life. They may not overtly look for this, less still admit it, but if you are an arty or intuitive type, something will click into place for Capricorn, like a secret combination lock.

There has to be a sense of appropriateness for this sign. You need to fit within their framework, because they will want to place you in their lives. So, if you like gadding about, performing chameleon changes, or have a hard time deciding which of your multiple personalities is the true you, then you will confuse

Capricorn's internal satnav and homing device which rely on you emitting a steady frequency.

If you're dating a Capricorn, you will be taken to their favourite haunts – there will be no surprises – and some Capricorns are particularly old-school and get so attached to their 'places' that you rarely see them outside of their club where they know exactly what to expect. Capricorns may not be the splashiest and flashiest people around. They dislike being obvious for a start. Going out is all about quality control and whether you are in their favourite pub or high-end restaurant they know what they like and the value of it.

If you are taking out a mountain goat, then make sure you've done your homework. Spontaneity is not their idea of a good time and causes Capricorn anxiety – what happens if there's no space for you? Or the timing doesn't work? Time and space are essentially Capricorn parameters and they prefer dates that are perfectly organised and orchestrated. It's best to know this right from the beginning so that you can plan accordingly!

They may not be the most relaxed company – unless you are true soulmates and feel the warm-up has been taken care of in previous lifetimes! Usually it takes a while to get to know your mountain goat. Their conversation may not venture into the personal domain. It might indeed be quite work-oriented. They can be shy, reserved and a little uptight – which is why you need to engage them in ways that allows them to drop some of their defensive veneer.

From this you could deduce that Capricorn is not exactly a bundle of laughs – but this sign has a fabulous sense of humour and many famous comedians are born under this sign. Beneath the po-face they have a dry wit, a sense of irony and the ridiculous. It's just that Capricorns have been taught from a young age to be mature and serious, and it's a hard habit to drop.

Capricorn takes love seriously too. They won't flirt and frolic with just 'anybody'. So, if you're getting these signals from the goat, then they really are interested in you. A Capricorn won't fake their feelings. If your goat tells you that they love you then they really mean it. It's for real. Isn't that worth a hundred of those people who will say anything that they think you want to hear?

Then there are some Capricorns that find the field of human intimacy rather scary. They have spent a lifetime building up protection against vulnerability. It's possible for them to gradually open their heart, but it might slam shut at the first hint of treachery. When Capricorn gives you the cold shoulder you will feel those ice blasts from Siberia. Being frozen out by Capricorn is a trip up the Matterhorn without thermals, that's for sure.

If, however, you've managed to melt those ice peaks then you'll be surprised at how comfortable Capricorn is in the realm of physical exchange. Being an Earth sign, the body is their comfort zone and it is often through physical affection that Capricorn speaks the non-verbal language of love. They do know how to give themselves body and soul and there is a realness about them. As they are so comfortable in the material realm of tangibles your Capricorn won't cut off distractedly, you won't feel as if they aren't there. It's possible to get to know who they are through touch. In fact, when you get up close and personal, you might even feel as if they are giving you the Earth.

Keeping: in it for the Long Haul

Commitment and Capricorn go together. Capricorns have a better understanding of what it means to commit than just about any other sign. The lead-up to this development is their expertise at monitoring 'where the relationship is going' from day one. You could be forgiven for thinking that you will be emailed a schedule with certain procedures that must be tackled in the correct order. Don't think for one minute that you're going to go into this without it all being thought out in advance. Capricorn practically invented 'the rules of engagement'.

So, it's unlikely that you get to be 'the one' for a Capricorn on the spur of the moment (unless there is a strong Air or Fire element in their chart). This will more likely be a decision that takes an enormous amount of input. Capricorn likes to do things properly, whether it's the asking or the doing.

They also have to be sure. Which means you have to be sure too. Dilly-dalliers and time-wasters need not apply. For Capricorn, marriage or commitment comes with attendant duties that involve creating solid financial roots from which your empire can be built. Make no mistake, even if it's an empire of just the two of you, in Capricorn's books it is as important as a huge conglomerate.

Entering into union with a Capricorn is akin to setting up a business partnership – perhaps the prenup has already made you aware of that! There can be something quite transactional about the Capricorn approach – you offer this and I offer that. Unromantic as it sounds, the mountain goat views your commitment to each other as a deal, with both sides aware of the small print, the contract and the consequences. At least you are with a grown-up! This is a very important point. Capricorns want to take care of you; they are responsible and have no problem shouldering the realities of the long journey, even if some of it is burdensome. This sign is clear-eyed and therefore they are not going to take issue when the going gets tough. They have that inner steely strength. Some of them seem to have granite at their core. Your Capricorn is not going to throw up their hands in horror at the first sign of trouble, much less fall apart. They are masters at overcoming difficulties and very few unions between any star sign avoid some time spent in the doldrums, so it's good to be with a professional fixer.

One issue that can be a theme in the coupledom of Capricorns is the parent-child syndrome. Capricorn is undoubtedly the parent and therefore often attracts an emotionally needier partner. This partner's ability to feel is like nectar to the buttoned-up goat who has always been told not to cry, from the cradle on. Inevitably, Capricorn has internalised their emotions, repressed them, sat on them – whatever was needed to be done in order for them not to come out, often at considerable cost to their wellbeing. This has turned them to stone in some cases. So when a soft, warm, emotionally available person comes into their lives Capricorn feels the manna from heaven, the permission to open up their heart from its locked-in state. Yet old habits die hard and too much dependency, emotional frailty and childlike neediness is repellent to this self-sufficient sign who can't understand how anyone could allow themselves to fall into a baby state. Capricorn is in control and they will try to control you AND your feelings if they deem them inappropriate. It's called tough love – and the boundaries the mountain goat puts in place can become a brick wall.

In a long-term relationship, the Capricornian type of resilience and affinity with permanence can be the glue that holds things together or the stultifying influence that causes a break down in the relationship. It all depends on your particular attachment style. Some partners absolutely thrive on the knowledge that Capricorn will stick things out, see them through and have the capacity to create something lasting. Others may enjoy an initial sense of security but feel restricted within the confines of the Capricorn playlist.

The mountain goat may not be starry-eyed about love and marriage, but they can deal with reality. There's a lot to be said for this. The Capricornian down-to-earth take on life cuts through illusion and anchors people to the real business of the relationship rather than the fantasy. There is perhaps less disappointment this way – if you never expected the full-blown rose garden then you can appreciate just having some solid ground.

Yet Capricorn has a tender side. It might be hidden, but it's there. They know how to nurture and protect you. They can sustain you through hard times, they can help you grow and develop – in fact, Capricorn unions thrive when both partners enjoy a great sense of purpose through their togetherness.

A stable home and personal life underpins Capricorn's exist-ence – so they appreciate a partner with the capacity to create strong foundations here. Capricorn is the 'parental guidance' sign, so having people under their wing brings out the best in them. It can be their own children who actively encourage the Capricorn parent to loosen up a little and be more playful. Capricorn likes to live in the best neighbourhood, to establish themselves as the pillar of the community, the respected head of the family or the 'best' mother or father. Capricorns possess a fervent desire to rise to the top and if you are with them then that includes you and the children. No shirkers!

So tying the knot is very meaningful to this sign, as the whole concept of being tethered seems entirely reasonable to them. Capricorn truly understands the concept of being in it for the long haul – anything less gives them the jitters. Those karmic ties and chords are something they choose to live with and are preferable than the free-floating freedom that some other signs crave. You see, Capricorn wishes for substance – so quick flings are never their route to satisfaction (unless there is Gemini or Aquarius in their chart). Perhaps their relationships are rather transactional in nature, or resemble an investment – but Capricorn wants to give you X and receive Y. It really is a simple equation if you do the maths!

The Ex Factor: Cutting the Ties That Bind
It takes a lot to end a relationship with a Capricorn. They are natural keepers and never enter or exit relationships without a great deal of forethought. One of the killers for them is if you treat them without respect, a word that might not figure large with other signs, but is an absolute requirement for Capricorn. There is always a core element of properness, something a little starchy about Capricorn. Treat them with disrespect and you will be tut-tutted as if they are Mary Poppins. Worse than that – damage will be done that makes Capricorn question if you are really truly serious about them or even about life. Both are cardinal sins in their books.

What might sour the relationship for the other person is the Capricorn resistance to emotional expression. They can be hard work in this department and essentially non-forthcoming. The mountain goat believes that people should 'manage' their feelings, be strong and stay on track – with their goals and achievements as the primary object of desire and fulfilment. This means that many Capricorns can go through the motions of being married without being fully engaged. Some remain remote and distant after decades of togetherness. Unsurprisingly, if you find yourself with one of those it can be emotionally lonely and besides that the Capricorn fixation on work means that business comes first.

If Capricorn decides it's over then they will absolutely create a business-deal end to the relationship. You might find you only talk to them again through their lawyers.

They are shrewd and sharp, finalising any settlement as if they are a born-again asset stripper. Perhaps not overly generous, but nevertheless they are realistic and know about fulfilling duties and obligations.

If you are the one who decides to go off-piste on your climb up the mountain with them, then Capricorn will soldier on alone. They are in fact very good on their own because they don't need others to fill their emotional needs. Capricorn will be sad, but will get on with their lives, stoically continuing without you.

DESTINY

The Capricorn Crew: the A-List

Capricorn is essentially loyal to friends and co-workers. They also like to maintain longevity here – with a lot of their associations going back many years, even to school days. It's all about the history – this means a lot to them and they see it as binding. Capricorns tend to seek out powerful connections – people who can smooth their path or give them the next leg up the ladder – never forget this is an upwardly mobile sign.

So it's not unusual to find the mountain goat in the rarefied atmosphere of the A-list or A-team. In fact, they know the secret pathways to achieving this status.

There is often something self-reliant about the life of a Capricorn – they can make do, they can carry on in extreme difficulty and as a model of how to keep calm in a crisis, Capricorn is hard to beat. However, they may feel down and they have a tendency towards pessimism – almost as an insurance policy against anything going wrong. In a team it is their voice that points out the pitfalls, that doesn't expect to automatically zoom to success. Yet, they are still standing when others have fallen. However long it takes, and this is a sign that plays the long game, the proof is in the pudding – that snow-peaked mountain top they intend to get to in the end. They love to build projects over the long term – generating a sense of purpose that glues people together. They tend not to view setbacks as permanent because they are naturally predisposed to looking at the end game and this can be a helpful perspective for those who get disheartened along the way.

In friendship they are stalwart, helping out the friend in need, providing a stabilising force for those who find themselves at the bottom of the barrel. Capricorn can let their hair down with their old friends, their trusted team members, and then you see the delight that Capricorn takes in enjoying shared experiences. They savour them, remember them and build on them. If you have a Capricorn friend you can count yourself lucky to know they are the opposite of the fair-weather kind. They really will be there for you.

CAPRICORN

♑

ALTAR OBJECTS

Place some of these objects on your altar or carry them with you in actual or pictorial form.

*

CRYSTAL: garnet, agate, black onyx

MINERAL/METAL: lead

CAPRICORN SYMBOLS: the Goat, Saturn (Chronos)

TAROT CARD: Judgement

ANGEL CARDS: Angel Hanael, Archangel Azrael

FLOWERS: holly, ivy, African violet, blue thistle

TREE: pine

SCENTS AND CANDLES: musk, leather, wood moss, basil, sage

MEMORY BOARD/PHOTOGRAPHS/PICTURES: mountains, 'old times', awards; painting: 'Saturn' by Jacob Matham (from The Planets)

CLOTH: wool in indigo

TALISMAN: heirloom

*

AQUARIUS

AQUARIUS

Avant-Garde Activists and Alternatives

CORE QUALITIES: *change makers, free spirited, intuitive, contradictory*

Mantra: Today I will reach for the highest, most ground-breaking answers.

The constellation of Aquarius: Aquarius is situated between Capricorn and Pisces. It is a large but fairly faint constellation with its brightest star being Beta Aquarii at 2.9 magnitude.

You can almost feel the air around you shift when you meet an Aquarian, as if someone has switched the air conditioning on. They get energies to circulate, they turn the heat down. It's easy to shoot the breeze with this friendly, seemingly open-minded sign – that is, until you say something they consider biased or high-handed. Pretty soon your Aquarian will blow a gale, bringing your house down with their mighty capacity to pop the bubble of self-righteousness. Even if you didn't think you were anything of the sort, Aquarius can take umbrage at your remarks, or take the opposing position just to spook you, to make you jump and see how you respond.

It's best never to take anything for granted when the water bearer is around. Their purpose in life is to shake things up a bit, so how can you possibly expect the status quo to remain as it is? You are in the presence of a revolutionary, even if they look as if butter wouldn't melt. It's all part of the surprise!

It's really not easy for Aquarius to 'fit in' with anything that operates on rules and conventions. Although they are brilliant with people and have a natural affinity with humanity, when they have to deal with protocols, structures and set-ups they just can't help wanting to tear it all down. Obviously not every water bearer is a renegade rebel, but they have the power to question all aspects of authority with one simple outside-of-the-box sentence.

You see, Aquarius lives in a different space/time continuum from other signs. You might say they live in a parallel universe. What is real to them is THE FUTURE. The past is done and dusted, why repeat it? Aquarius wants to introduce the new, make a difference, move things along, and they get impatient with those who doggedly refuse to reinvent the wheel.

They are the water bearers – but not to be confused with a water sign. Aquarius is all air, all abstract adventure. For them, the watery realm of feelings and intimacy is scary and best avoided – in case they lose their highly prized freedom and independence. So what is the water bearer bringing and pouring? It is the gift of knowledge. They channel ideas directly from a higher source and then pour them out in a form that nurtures humanity.

LIFE

Health

If feelings are potentially a danger zone for this lofty sign, then the body is another realm that threatens to imprison them. Aquarius lives mainly in their head – the realm of ideas and communication is what fuels them – and some can have difficulty taking time to properly honour the body, feel comfortable in it and attend to its needs. Then there is the other type of super-healthy Aquarian who is fired up by the latest dietary fad or machine or who enjoys the group element of exercise and is constantly at the gym, pool, pitch or class.

Mind

As Aquarius is always mentally one step ahead of the game, it's often hard to understand where they're coming from, let alone keep up. It's a common experience for Aquarians to be derided for concepts that are considered completely weird, only for them to be considered normal a few years down the line. What others deem 'alternative' about the Aquarius mindset becomes main-stream. It's almost as if Aquarius shines a light on what's going to unfold. They are the torch bearers.

Mentally, they can be contrary and contradictory – posing the opposite viewpoint is entirely natural to them. One of the reasons they do this is to get some space, as they dislike people being subjective and prefer a wide-angle lens through which they can see the whole picture. Aquarians are also markedly brilliant with original thought. They question everything and formulate free-thinking that turns the accepted way of doing things on its head.

Body

If the water bearer has learned to truly inhabit their body, then they have earthed their high-frequency wiring and can generate electricity. Otherwise, you get the feeling that Aquarius has not fully incarnated, is not completely downloaded and is hovering somewhere above their body in the ethers, which accounts for the faraway look in their eyes.

As with electricity, they can be high or low voltage and either super wired up or flat-line wiped out. Aquarius needs to learn to stabilise their circuits. The areas of the body they are connected to are the legs, ankles and circulatory system. Movement is key to their wellbeing.

Spirit

As Aquarians operate on another plane – the fifth dimension instead of the earthly third – they can often appear to be 'above it all'. Not that they consider themselves to be better than anyone else, but they would prefer not to engage with the uncivilised ego-behaviour that permeates planet Earth. They keep a distance, do not get involved in petty squabbles and remain far removed from the daily irritants and interactions that drive mere mortals to distraction.

Spiritually and Karmically

Within the next 300 years we will enter the Age of Aquarius and are already acclimatising to Aquarius: our technology is speeding up the rate of evolution and we are trying to evolve our human consciousness in order to save the planet and help humanitarian

300 Written in the Stars

crises. Aquarius is the sign that works best in groups, that feels connected to the world at large, that is outraged by the drive for personal gain at the expense of other people. The planet Uranus is the ruler of Aquarius. This planet is all about cutting-edge development, radical breakthroughs that are made in politics and society; they are the mavericks – the karma of Aquarius is to be a vehicle for this to happen in however small or big a way.

What Does Aquarius Have to Give?

Aquarius presents us with a different take on life. Their capacity to act as a one-person pop-up wakes us up from complacency and makes us reconsider our views, values and way of life. Sometimes Aquarius will use shock tactics to deliberately disarm us with their non-conformist approach. However, not all Aquarians are walking hand grenades, but gentle souls whose intent is to broaden our minds – or at least make us question what we are doing.

It is almost as if Aquarius is there to show us that what passes for normal these days is perhaps not the best way. Even so, they receive a lot of flack from more conventional, conservative types who defend their position by declaring the water bearer to be a nutjob. Aquarius is unruffled and will carry on in their own sweet way, defying the rut so that they can forge a new path. There is a kind of brilliance about Aquarius; they can be magician-like, pulling rabbits from hats whilst at the same time erratically wobbling on their own frequency.

Aquarius shows us there is another way to be. As the sign of friendship, they rise above the high jinks of personal drama and demonstrate how to operate from a more objective place, one where there is care and concern but everyone is given personal liberty to do their own thing.

What Does Aquarius Need to Receive?
Their cool-as-a-cucumber approach is great for defusing difficulties, but Aquarius needs to enter the realm of personal love. If their world has become a bit like a science lab – which might be perfect for their experiments – it probably lacks the intimacy that can only be born of shared warmth and feelings.

It is in the arena of relationships that the water bearer has to open up to the same indignities, suffering and confusion as anyone else and experience some of the mysteries of human foibles and responses. This is where the Aquarian addiction to 'being reasonable' meets its match. The hotbed of human emotion can be anything but reasonable, plunging the water bearer into temperatures and depths that are totally out of their comfort zone, yet teach them how to engage with the heart.

Often Aquarius attracts people who require a huge amount of attention and this puts them on the hot/cold axis where neither partner feels at peace. Ultimately, Aquarius seeks friendship as the basis for any other kind of connection. Yet, although hiding out within the group and pouring all that water into so many different people may feel good, it keeps them at a distance from an all-important one-to-one connection. This is the thing that will really bring them in from the cold.

As Aquarians thrive on the surprise element, loving to do things on the spur of the moment, they live spontaneously – which has its merits. Yet they can fall through the cracks and actually miss out on achieving by means of an ordered or structured plan.

Some Aquarians really need to be brought down to earth by a more grounded type of person. Life lessons can bring the maturity of dealing with the everyday 'stuff' instead of fixating on what is extraordinary. Someone who is good at 'keeping things going' can help Aquarius to settle and stabilise.

What Does Aquarius Need to Learn?
This future-oriented sign can live life on fast forward, never having time to savour the now or to acknowledge that the past may have value. Putting things in context is important, as is recognising that other people may be so resistant to change that they find it threatening. Whilst the water bearer adores living on the edge of excitement, many of the other signs hate the idea of not knowing what's going to happen next. For all the Aquarian open-mindedness, they can be rather closed to other people's fears, failing to recognise that fear is also there for a reason.

This is where the Aquarian impersonal approach has its own limitations. Their stubbornness – and Aquarius as a fixed sign can become overwhelmingly stuck with their own principles – becomes a barrier to true connection and especially to intimacy, which can be the one thing that terrifies this sign as it means they must engage with feelings that threaten to submerge them and close the exit doors to their personal freedom.

Idealistic by nature, Aquarius wishes that everyone could tune in to the needs of the world at large, the planet or a project, rather than their own requirements. Aquarius has causes where other signs have personal concerns. They live macro whilst others are attuned to micro. Aquarians can galvanise teams into action and fight for justice where inequality and inhumanity exist – yet paradoxically they sometimes lack compassion. It would be good if they could view things from the other side, and acknowledge that humans should give equal credence to emotional as well as intellectual intelligence, so the head and the heart can be balanced.

LOVE

Dating – or Just Friends?

For Aquarians, the whole dating process is indistinguishable from their driving force to gather friends. As the water bearer collects contacts, navigates networks and is a huge team player, they often grow closer to someone with whom they already hang out or share a mutual interest. Crossing the line is a dance in and out between the friendship and romantic interest. It can actually be difficult to know if the Aquarian likes you 'in that way' because they tend to treat you the same whether you're a great love or a member of their gym!

Curiosity is the quality that sparks their interest. Aquarius sniffs out something interesting about you and suddenly they're orbiting around you. It's elliptical – of course, the water bearer would never do anything normal. They bear down upon you, even asking seemingly insane and intrusive questions but then back off and you don't hear from them for weeks. You wonder if there's been a power cut. In a sense there may have been and you just have to get used to the electrical short-circuiting which is a main feature of this sign. It can drive the needy types crazy as there is nothing reassuringly predictable about where this relationship might go. Aquarius can pick you up and drop you, come in and out of your life, act super keen and then detached. If you can withstand the quick changes and can see beyond their need to step back and forth, if you believe you have something special enough to make this person worth your while, then it can turn out to be the most amazing connection you will ever have.

Aquarians don't do drama, or game-playing. They have no time for emotional scenes or ultimatums. At least on that level things are relatively straightforward. It's just the friend thing. The answer is: be their friend! What other quality would better underpin your love?

So if your Aquarian is acting cool as a cucumber, somewhat cut off and distant, is refusing to admit you are a couple and nothing more intimate has passed between you than a comment on the weather, then it's best to not take it personally. Use the space they give you to Be You! After all, this is really what they're attracted to – and they will come back, curious as ever, wanting to know more, to be with you, to do new things together. Even if they've invited other people along 'to make up the numbers'. Ha! You know that old safety trick. It's fine. If you are tuned into Aquarius you'll recognise and realise it's the shared glance, the careless arm over your shoulder, the unmistakeable frisson in the air (remember the electricity that surrounds Aquarius) and you'll know that those other people are purely a safety blanket designed to provide some padding, whilst the water bearer gets used to the idea that their heart is pounding, their feelings are surfacing and they WANT YOU! If and when things do get intimate between you, the water bearer crackles with energy and can be pretty disinhibited.

Aquarians can blindside you with their views on commitment and relationships. Essentially they will support any way of maintaining their independence. Being in a relationship with you has to be a choice, not a given.

Obviously, Aquarius is not going to do the dating game as other people might do it. The romantic dinners, plenty of private time *a deux*, the checking in before and after – no. That's for those insecure types who can't live their own lives (in the mind of an Aquarian, who will make up the dating rules as they go along). At least they will be tailor-made for you on every occasion

– so just as you are getting the hang of them, Aquarius turns tail, sidesteps in the opposite direction, and you really don't know where you are.

Similarly, if you are hoping to entice a water bearer, do not follow your tried-and-tested formula. Aquarians may not be 'romantic' in the old-fashioned sense of the word, but they believe in soulmates, karmic connections and twin flames – they've read all about cosmic consciousness and you'd do well to have this kind of information up your sleeve. It might even help them return your text – if you can intrigue them enough without scaring them off.

Best to keep things light and interesting and, above all, remember that you have to demonstrate you can manage perfectly well without them. There is nothing more suffocating to an Aquarian than the person who swamps them emotionally, with huge expectations that send the water bearer running for the hills.

Conversation must range across a huge variety of subjects and they respect you for having your own opinions – especially if they can polarise with them and encourage a mutual combustion that means you both learn something.

If there is something unusual about your meeting, a juxtaposition of cultures, age, backgrounds or interests then so much the better as the water bearer likes to cross great divides – it's all extra stimulation.

The water bearer can pride themselves on choosing to be with the one person everyone else considers unsuitable, the person no one expected them to be with. However, if you are from the same mould then the magic sparkle-dust of friendship can create the attraction Aquarius craves.

Some water bearers are simply not cut out for long-term

togetherness in that couple-y way – it makes them shiver. Perhaps they are once bitten, twice shy but they function best when they have their own space and place. If you are dating a water bearer, you might feel they continually challenge all laws of attachment: baulking at being called your girlfriend or boyfriend, never letting you know where you stand or when you're going to see them next. It's all part of the Aquarian style . . . it takes a lot of ingenuity for you to find a way to attach with detachment – but this is the answer.

Keeping . . . the Spark Alive
Captivating the Aquarian interest for a moment is easy. Keeping it is not. Many of their long-term relationships hit the skids because of the sheer routine and mundane conformity that got in the way of the Aquarian dream. As Aquarians tend to believe that any kind of occasion is a commercial enterprise where good people are exploited by big business, don't expect them to go down the route of a formalised grand event. Aquarius would rather the two of you just took off together; unless it is a wedding party with friends, then Aquarius would rather not play. They certainly don't want your old boss or Great Aunt Amelia to be watching your first dance.

Strangely, underneath their seemingly detached manner, Aquarians are hugely sensitive and can startle like deer. You have to bear this in mind if you're attempting to get them near the altar. Maybe you are old friends who turned things around after decades and decided to tie the knot, or people who met on a plane six weeks ago. Whatever the nature of your union, Aquarius will want to do things their way. With or without ceremony.

Settling into your partnership? Well, don't get too comfortable as your water bearer is likely to want to reinvent the whole thing from time to time. It will be like having several marriages to the same person – at least it keeps things interesting! The water bearer likes to be kept on their toes, not with drama, but through discovering something new – so if the two of you can maintain that wide-eyed interest in the world and all it has to offer then so much the better. Underlying the whole partnership, of course, must be that vital ingredient of friendship, shared ideals and lots of personal freedom.

Domesticity doesn't appeal too much to Aquarius, who tends to view mundane matters as burdensome and boring; to be got through so that life can be lived on a more exciting plane. They also like to have an open-house policy, so don't think you're going to cosy up together that much. Having friends over or having them to stay for extended periods, using the home as a place for get-togethers, makes sense to Aquarius who needs the constant stream of people in order to thrive.

Obviously, if you prefer a very quiet life then Aquarius is not for you. But if you're thinking of getting hitched to your water bearer don't expect them to change too much from the sociable, people-oriented person you first met.

There is another side to Aquarius – the loner. They like to counteract the constant throng with 'time out' – which means time alone, just for themselves. Time to do exactly as they please, and this does not include your company. Don't be offended. It's not a rejection of you, but a reconnection to themselves. Some Aquarians can go into a hermit-like place, cut off from the outside world. They do inhabit two contrasting spaces – one which is filled with other people, the other which is their own personal zone, marked KEEP OUT. As you can see, life with an Aquarian partner is not everyone's cup of water! However, you will never be bored. Aquarius is young at heart, immensely interested and interesting. There's a lot to be said for the liveliness of their energy, their refusal to bow down to conformity and live as others think they should. In fact, others may see you together as being semi-detached rather than fully paired-up, but you have to actually be with an Aquarian to experience that special electricity between you that surpasses all the cloistered intimacy and expectation that characterises other kinds of relationships.

Aquarius will also allow you to be yourself. This is not to be underestimated – many partnerships that become two halves of a whole are dedicated to being perfect mirrors. People can lose themselves in that kind of relationship. Aquarius will give you just the same level of space they accord themselves and this can be a great gift and blessing. Imagine being able to be you whilst having a really exciting partner. You won't have to make the kinds of compromises people routinely make because with Aquarius there are no oughts and no shoulds.

It's not that you end up with just a flatmate or a friend with benefits; Aquarius perhaps understands the nature of your 'special relationship' more than other signs – respecting your individuality and not standing in the way of what's important for you. This can be a great support. If you are a clinging vine then Aquarius will prune away your hooks. They simply can't tolerate any form of suffocation, but they are essentially considerate and kind and they have a sensitivity that intuitively registers where you're at – a form of psychic radar that picks up on the non-verbal as they constantly scan the airwaves for information. They may not offer you tea and sympathy when you have a problem, but they can jolt you out of it, simply by offering an entirely new angle on it. How wonderful is that!

As a parent, Aquarius likes to be the role model that enables their offspring to stand on their own two feet. They encourage independence, creative thinking and are thrilled to explore unusual interests and activities. The Aquarian parent may have a problem fitting into the school system, questioning the need for this or that, but they are loyal champions of their children, making sure they engage with the world.

So Aquarius as a long-term partner is not mission impossible, but nevertheless a challenge to the concept of being tied down. If you can learn the art of hanging loose and flying the freedom flag with them, then you will be treated to a loyalty that comes from them constantly choosing to be with you.

You may find yourself with them in a semi-detached relationship that lasts for decades longer than other people's more conventional unions. This in itself makes the water bearer chuckle, 'Who said it wouldn't last?' The more unlikely it looks, the better!

For some partners, the constant comings and goings of friends and acquaintances, being treated as if you are a casual contact at times rather than the chosen one, is beyond the pale. But if you can stick with it, you will see that the friendship you have between you is the very thing that makes your union so special.

The Ex Factor: Over and Out!
As Aquarians are not especially keen on 'the piece of paper' associated with marriage – feeling affronted by the conformity of it – many prefer not to legalise unions. However, if your love story

has come to an end, the heartbreak is the same with or without the paper to tear up and the divorce to go through.

If the water bearer has totally lost interest in maintaining your union, then you will be subject to their cut-and-dried approach. Their detachment is all too obvious and the water bearer can turn their back on you, almost as if your love never existed. They move on to the next chapter. Yet many do wish to remain friends as this was no doubt the basis for your relationship in the first place.

Leaving your Aquarian, on the other hand, means that you must explain yourself. Aquarius will want to know exactly what's going on in your mind and may well believe they can argue the point and turn it around. For those who always felt somewhat sidelined by Aquarius, who longed for greater intimacy than the water bearer was able to give, this is a powerful turning of the tables. Often at this point, Aquarius finally recognises that the heart can win over the head. No amount of cerebral companionship can fill the gap if someone feels unloved.

Of course, Aquarius can revert back to being on their own relatively easily, supplanting what your presence provided with a revolving door of friends. Usually, walking away from each other is with the minimum of fuss and fireworks. Aquarius wants to be reasonable, to be fair and adapt to the change without having to resort to angry or underhand tactics they would consider beneath them. For them it is a new age, to be embraced.

DESTINY

Friends Forever – the Aquarian Tribe

Who wouldn't want to be part of the Aquarian tribe? To be with the person who is made for friendship, group dynamics, teamwork and hive activity?

There is no other sign as advanced in their understanding of how people can thrive together than this one. The water bearer is innately open and adores to meet new people, and is the least stuffy and the most interested in those from all walks of life. All creeds, ethnicities, age groups and backgrounds are welcome – Aquarius loves to mix things up and can't understand why people choose to stick with a single clan or category when there are so many interesting differences to explore.

Digital and social media has also made it easier for Aquarius to reach out to an even broader spectrum of people and as everything virtual appeals to them, giving them instant access without the mundane mechanics of face-to-face meetings, the Aquarius can be permanently plugged in and linked up in the way they like to be.

Aquarius will even put together a family of friends with whom they forge closer connections than their actual blood ties. It goes with the Aquarian sensibility of creating their own context. A natural team player, this sign enjoys being part of a group that has formed through mutual interest. They can sense the mental frequency in the ether and how everyone's brainwaves align (a scientifically proven fact that is nectar for water bearers).

Aquarius will initiate gatherings, group holidays, meetings and events that are marker points for people to engage with something other than their immediate family life. It is as if they flag up the possibility of living as one big human family. This in itself can be a breath of fresh air for those struggling with personal relationships as it offers them freedom and escape and connection with like-minded people – a lifeline for some.

Aquarius understands team spirit, promotes it and actively wants each person to play to their strengths. Whether in a corporate setting, a sports team, a yoga class or a social event, this is the sign who will do the joined-up thinking for the group, connect everyone and neutralise dominant egos so that everybody benefits.

AQUARIUS

ALTAR OBJECTS

Place some of these objects on your altar or carry them with you in actual or pictorial form.

*

CRYSTAL: yellow jasper, crystal, aquamarine

MINERAL/METAL: aluminium

AQUARIUS SYMBOL: water in a hand

TAROT CARD: The Star

ANGEL CARDS: Angel Mihr, Archangel Uriel

FLOWERS: arum Lily, azalea, iris

TREE: bonsai

SCENTS AND CANDLES: aloe, tangerine, lime

MEMORY BOARD/PHOTOGRAPHS/PICTURES: pictures from the Hubble Space Telescope, friends, groups and social activities; painting: 'Creation of Adam' by Michelangelo.

CLOTH: ribbon of electric blue, ultramarine

TALISMAN: found object, lucky skull

*

PISCES

PISCES

Angel Fish and Piranhas

CORE QUALITIES: *soulful, intuitive, empathic, self-sacrificing, avoidant*

Mantra: Today I will remember that having boundaries will support me.

The constellation of Pisces: Pisces lies between Aquarius to the west and Aries to the East. It is one of the largest constellations in the sky, but contains no bright stars.

The two fish that swim in opposite directions are in fact a single unit that reaches both for the highs and lows in life. Why would anyone want to do that? Because Pisces seeks totality, wholeness, and therefore embraces the whole gamut of human experience. As the final sign on the circle of the zodiac, Pisces is a composite of the whole range of human possibilities. It's not surprising the fishes wonder who they are – the capacity to get lost in the oceanic wave is so great.

Pisces has an ability to surrender to whatever or whomever is presented. At first glance this may look like a weakness – especially if viewed from the me-first point of view of Aries, at the start of the zodiacal wheel. However, there is a saying: 'the strong one gives in'. Pisces is able to accept things without imposing their ego or will which is an enormous spiritual strength. The fish won't waste time battling things out but looks for a way to neutralise, escape or opt out of tension. Very sensible indeed!

Brimming with emotional intelligence, Pisces looks for clues in the invisible, intangible, intuitive and emotional realm of life, trusting this realm more than anything the rational, material world can offer. Pisces is all about subtlety; they see the unseen, psychically read what is going on and swim the currents accordingly. Aligning with the cosmos, the universe, is actually a fine art – one that Pisces is here to master. To the outside world it looks like they live on the line of least resistance. Never stubbornly holding on, like Taurus, or attempting to control the outcome with imposed order like Virgo. Pisces lets things wash over them, they coast, they float, they go with the flow.

Yet every sign has its attributes and sore spots. For Pisces, they can reach the heights of spiritual awareness and inspiration or become a victim of their own unwillingness to step into ego – they become lost, confused and trampled upon. It is Pisces' choice whether they swim high or low and how they integrate all they have learned so that they gain insight from even their greatest disappointments and let-downs.

Pisceans literally yearn to be taken away from all this – the mundane ordinariness that stifles the magic they're looking for. This sign spins fantasies and has an affinity with all that is surreal, numinous and mystical. The romantic nature of Pisces lends a tremendous openness to their very being. They love the special effects, loathe the drab bleakness of a harsher, starker reality. Yet, of course, they have to live in this earthly world and deal with its physical goods. If they can download their dream to the material world then it's possible for them to actually live it.

Pisces fits in anywhere, with a chameleon-like capacity to know whatever is required in any situation and then match it. They are rarely out of place and if they find themselves to be a fish out of water they can become invisible, disappear into their own space. However, they can also live their lives in a bubble – floating in the air, somehow not of this world, not fully present because the veil between worlds is so thin to their eyes that they can see through it and participate in both simultaneously – a more extra-ordinary act than anything the Cirque du Soleil can perform!

LIFE

Health

Pisces rules the feet – appropriate for their need to be grounded. As a sign they can be so open that their physical body receives all that is in the atmosphere – including viruses, colds, bad moods and sadness. Often Pisces 'picks up' physical ailments or emotions that begin with someone else. They absorb them into themselves and have to learn to transmute them or develop a higher level of protection and defence.

Mind

Pisces has a direct line to the superconscious realm and therefore access to higher wisdom. This is how they seemingly pluck answers from out of the air or can 'tune in' and come up with something no one else has thought of. Their intuitive guidance is a blessing, yet Pisces can have a hard time with linear thinking and cold hard facts. If there is no subtle meaning then Pisces finds it hard to understand   they can literally get stuck on Level One. This is why they may suffer in the educational system – gliding through it with their head in the clouds but unable to tick the boxes that school demanded of them.

When it comes to imagination, few other signs can surpass the sheer poetry of Pisces. Many Pisceans have a gift for translating the ordinary into the beautiful, for capturing images and conveying glamour by adding a bit of sheen and sparkle. Pisces may not be the most confident in terms of expression, but the value of their thoughts is immense.

They also telepathically know what you are thinking without you even saying a word. Pisces is master of the non-verbals. Even if you are speaking, they can read between the lines, get the nuance and the underlying feelings. With their highly sensitised radar that is open to everything in the airwaves, the fish is delicately poised to receive everything that surrounds them. Even if it is too much information! They learn mainly through osmosis, soaking things up in a sponge-like way. Unsurprisingly it can be almost impossible for them to explain how they know what they know.

Body

There is often something luminous about Pisces. They do give off a seductive aura but often look as if they are not actually in their body, as if they could fly out of it or are already hovering in the air. As Pisces' greatest strength is emotional and spiritual, they have to work hard at even finding the physical plane interesting enough to inhabit. They don't want to feel trapped in the corporeal realm with all its limitations. So Pisces glistens and glimmers, is innately brilliant at evoking physically glamorous images, but when it comes to the daily grind of diet, sleep and exercise this has to be learned.

Spirit

Pisces is so attuned to the spirit, even if they do not make a big song and dance about it, they exude a healing presence. Their compassion and empathy, their ability to put themselves in your shoes, gives them a huge connection line to other people. This is a wonderful thing. Yet, many Pisceans feel wiped out, overwhelmed and overloaded because they are quite simply receiving too much from others – not all of which is a gift.

Spiritually and Karmically

The ruling planet of Pisces is Neptune, god of the sea. Water dissolves solid matter and is a substance that can change shape from still to stormy to white-water rapids. Pisces' energy can either be the refreshing effervescence of a fountain or a deluge, a torrent, that threatens to swamp dry land.

However, water is clever and always finds a way around obstacles, either by eroding, climbing over or under. Seeping through defences – aha – this is how Pisces can get to you!

This sign has a natural connection to the divine, whatever their religion or even if they are agnostic. Their connection to the Source remains. Their life path often requires them to develop reserves of trust and faith in life itself or in some kind of divine order. The theme of loss can be a big one for Pisceans. The nature of this loss can be material, emotional or both, but Pisces has to find redemption, to remain intact even in the face of suffering. The hopefulness of the Piscean spirit is a wonder, but the loss of hope is often a portal into greater wisdom and understanding where Pisces is cast adrift and has to find themselves and their belief in life. Call it grace, but some Pisceans transmute incredible pain into something sublime.

What Does Pisces Have to Give?

Pisces has so much to offer when it comes to modelling an alternative response to the demands of living in the mundane material world. One of their greatest gifts is to help make things bearable for other people. They know how to console, comfort and reassure those who are having problems. They are the sign that is most adept at accepting the unacceptable because their capacity to surrender is second to none. As we build great defences against ever having to experience loss, even though we all know that loss is inevitable, Pisces understands the conundrum here and can gently help someone cope when the illusion that they will never lose anything dear to them shatters.

Their natural affinity to work with the law of attraction – by having a fully functioning wish list – is also pretty impressive. Pisces may not go all out to get something like a Fire sign would. Their modus operandi is simpler than that. They just connect to their dream and magnetise it into being. Perhaps more than any other sign, Pisces is able to magic up a minor, or even a major, miracle!

They are also very good at inspiring others to look beyond the ordinary world – to remember there is a lot more mystery to life than our technology-based, rational, reasonable mindset appreciates. When we don't know the answer, Pisces can help us live with that. They can coast along in uncertain territory and relieve us of the need to always know exactly what we want, what is going on, or what will happen in any given situation.

So, if Pisces can soften our outlook, create more romance and inspiration, then we are the richer for it. For all their drifting, Pisces can teach us to let go of the incredible urge to seize control. For Pisces, holding things lightly, being equally skilled with what is lost or found, is a great lesson. One that tallies with the Buddhist Law of Impermanence.

Through Pisces we recognise the layers and complexities of life and how easy it is to get lost in them or to assume something is what it appears to be, without checking with our intuition.

What Does Pisces Need to Receive?

As Pisces swims around in their ethereal perception they do need someone to point out the logistics of the mundane world. It's not that all Pisceans are hopelessly chaotic but they tend to fantasise, dream and romanticise. Their longing for the ideal means they sometimes overlook some of the starker realities. In worst case scenarios, Pisces is in denial about the truth, deluding themselves into believing something is the way they want it to be rather than the way it actually is.

Being gently pulled down to earth is good for Pisces, as long as they feel they have access to their bubble of bliss should they want to visit!

Pisces also needs to develop boundaries, so having them yourself can be a useful role model. The shock of coming up against the No word can wake Pisces up to the possibility that they too can separate themselves out from over-giving, from identifying with other people's needs at their own expense. Even being asked what they want can throw Pisces! They are so adaptable, being a mutable sign, that they are able to contort themselves to meet any shape required and therefore what they themselves want is often the last thing they can get hold of. Sometimes they literally haven't got a clue what they want . . .

More than anything, perhaps, Pisces needs to receive love, tenderness and understanding. They are gentle people who can get hurt by the snatch-and-grab attitude of those who are on their own mission to have life revolve around them. It's not much wonder that Pisces sometimes beats a retreat back into their own secluded world, their own dream where their fantasy realm protects them from the harshness of everyday life and interaction.

What Does Pisces Need to Learn?

As each and every sign has its own soul mission, Pisces perhaps more than any other sign is aware of the mysterious element to life that orchestrates synchronicity. They are very well attuned to the phenomenon of aligning themselves to the divine plan, the universal energy. They find it easier to master this than most other people, yet they can be fatalistic – giving up if they don't receive the symbols and signs that 'things are meant to be'. Their soul journey requires them to integrate their affinity with the numinous with a purposeful owning of their own ego and self.

All the letting go that Pisces performs can in the end lessen their grip on the third dimension, resulting in addictive behaviour, dissolution and victim status. Suffering is a big experience for Pisces. They will give their hearts to those who need help, but there is a kind of ecstatic agony mixed up in their own suffering – a hook that the fish can writhe and wriggle on for years if they don't learn how to put a stop to it.

It all boils down to knowing they have a choice. They can choose to abandon themselves to the vagaries of life, or choose to skilfully use their gifts and talents to accomplish what they were born to do.

LOVE

Dating: the Romantic Dream

If you like going fishing then you will already have some experience of the patience and stillness required in order to attract a fish! There may be plenty of fish in the sea, but your Pisces is clever at avoiding and escaping the catch. The dance between you is something that can be pure magic – your longing to have them, and their own curiosity about what you have got on your hook.

Pisces yearns for romance but is probably the most elusive and avoidant sign on the planet. In every cell of their being lies ambivalence as they twist and turn through the ever-changing waters of their existence. Should they or shouldn't they? Pisces may be in love with love, but dating a real human being is another matter. This is difficult enough to get a handle on, but the extraordinary thing about them is that they appear to be so very available! Aha – all that glitters is not gold . . . That flash of promise can dangle just out of reach.

However, as every experienced Fisher King knows, if you wait and don't freak out, you will eventually pique the interest of the fish who will come to you. Even if you've had to put your waders on this can be worth all the effort! Pisces is a charming date – able to talk about absolutely anything, to fit in absolutely anywhere. What's not to like?

Pisces can mirror you with astounding skill. This is why you can feel as if you have so much in common, that they completely 'get' you. Whatever territory you venture into, Pisces is capable of adapting the conversation to you so that nothing is awkward or uncomfortable. Merging is their special quality and pretty soon you will feel as if you've known them all your life. They literally slip into your presence, all shimmering subtle energy that is born of tremendous empathy and emotional intelligence.

Pisces is a natural healer and capable of uplifting your spirits, creating a seductive space where you are recognised, valued and understood. However, if you take a Pisces somewhere where the vibe isn't right then you will see their receptors go flat. Pisces can somehow disappear whilst standing right in front of you. In big crowds, noisy locations, around strident people, the fish swims away right in front of your eyes, even though to all intents and purposes they are going nowhere. The far-away look in their eyes says it all.

So think romance, if you are dating a Pisces. Where can you take them that is brimming with atmosphere – preferably somewhere that can transport them to another realm, where their creative juices can flow. Movies, theatre and performance are all big pluses and portals for opening up the Pisces heart chakra. Places to eat that offer something exotic, intimate and atmospheric are going to win over somewhere loud, busy and impersonal.

If you've attracted the attention of a Pisces and the hook is on the other fin so to speak then be prepared to hang loose on the logistics of the date. Pisces may prefer to ask you where you would like to go – it all goes with the mirroring. As the most commitment-phobic of signs they may not be able to make a plan well in advance but hold several alternatives open. There are times when the Piscean inability to choose and commit means they leave it so late that nowhere has availability! But if you're still interested, it doesn't really matter where you go – because the experience is all about being with them, even if you end up walking around town and grabbing a late-night bite wherever happens to be open.

If you date a Piscean you have to factor in a certain amount of chaos and confusion. You will soon realise that they can live without a defined plan. In fact, such a thing makes them nervous and can send them spinning away from you. Make no attempt to control them, pin them down or hook them. Just hold your ground and slowly, gently they will swim towards you.

Pisceans exude a magnetic energy that is indefinable, ethereal and enticing. For some signs the mermaid, magical quality remains ever-entrancing. For others frustration sets in as they realise they are dating a chameleon who changes colour to match their surroundings. It is hard for some signs to grasp a person who is not wholly, substantially emitting a strong version of themselves.

An added complication is the sense that Pisces doesn't know what or whom they are looking for until they find it. They may not even see YOU all that clearly because to them you are a Knight in Shining Armour or a Perfect Princess. Are they easy-going in overlooking your faults or do they not even see them in the first place? Pisces is capable of dating an idealised version of you for weeks, months or even years. Equally, they can create mirages around themselves that present an image rather than a reality. Is this a manipulation? Is it conscious or unconscious? Only you can decide that – it is best to go in with your eyes wide open.

Pisces has a terror of abandonment (even withstanding their commitment phobia – yes, it's complicated!). They can attach themselves to you in their idealised fantasy world and then appear clingy if you seem like you're getting away. This is in stark contrast to their own avoidant behaviour that has them stringing you along whilst they keep their other options (or dates) open. As you can see, dating a Pisces is never going to be a simple or straight-forward operation. You have to be able to live on several levels at once, deal with nuance, contradiction and confusion.

Another big theme for Pisces is rescue. They are attracted to those whom they can save, the 'misunderstood' person – or Pisces can need a lot of help themselves. Playing the damsel in distress or the lost cause comes naturally to them and if you're on that co-dependent frequency you can get trapped into running round after them, attempting to fix them. Pisces does like to be looked after, no doubt about it. Even when dating don't be surprised if Pisces suddenly needs you to drop everything and be there for them. There is a vulnerability to Pisces, sometimes a helpless element that asks for you to sort them out.

However, many Pisceans with self-sufficient factors in their charts are perfectly capable of managing their lives with or without you. This kind inspires you to reach for the stars, to dip into the magic in their company. Just being with them is so intoxicating you get a special access pass to Cloud Nine.

Keeping . . . Living the Dream
So your dreamboat wants to settle down . . . how do you make the magic last when you are either living with or marrying a fish? The more fantastic the dream, the more grounded you need to be about the reality of the everyday. Pisces is emotionally easy to live with despite their propensity to leave everything lying around and forgetting to do things! Of course there are exceptions – those who are neat-nick list-makers and cupboard tidiers – but in general the Pisces capacity to let go means that the practical domestics are not top of their priorities. The upside to being with Pisces is that they are so accommodating by nature, shape-shifting to suit your lifestyle,

prepared to move anywhere (although near to water is definitely their ideal).

You can live the romantic dream, blissed out. Stage a week-long love-fest without getting dressed, create candle-lit dinners, tantric togetherness, take exotically oiled and perfumed baths together. But when the rose petalled sheets needs changing – someone has to do the dirty work. This is not Pisces's bag – they are more come hither than come clean.

Pisces believes wholeheartedly in love – they can get very high on romance and the idea of soulmates. It can be hard then if they get to a point where they realise their soulmate is the one who is here to teach them the biggest karmic lesson. Sticking around, even when the going gets tough, is a huge evolutionary task for the fish. The daily grind literally grinds them down so they need the glitter of romance to be generously sprinkled in order to keep the magic alive.

The emotional connection between you must continue, preferably in as rapturous a mode as the day you first met, as closing off to a Pisces causes heartbreak. This is no mean feat – an impossible one even. You may not even recognise your mate is lovelorn as they are so good at masking what's wrong. Instead it manifests as physical symptoms, irritating indirectness or other avoidant, escapist means.

As long as there's something to captivate their imagination, their heart and soul, then Pisces pours all their love into maintaining your union. They have to have a dream – the dream home, perfect children . . . Creating happy-ever-after is a beautiful promise and sometimes Pisces has to adapt their expectations to being in a good place, rather than being ecstatic.

Merging is one of Pisces's specialities. The whole concept of being a twosome, joining everything together, is easily done. They operate fusion at its highest level. However, some unions go south if they are loaded with too much dependency and neediness; the partner is driven away to find their own sense of self again, which to Pisces smacks of abandonment – their number one nemesis. Pisces is pretty good at unconsciously manipulating you into staying with them. Although, of course, you might be in marriage heaven, entranced and enchanted and very happy to live in the bubble.

Keeping a Pisces requires you to tend to them, to be a caring person with a capacity to look beyond the ordinary to the extra-ordinary. The fish can hypnotise and mesmerise you – isn't that surreal? You will be living at Hogwarts, that's for sure!

The Ex Factor: Slinging your Hook

If Pisces feels utterly let down and disappointed, before you know it they can swim off in the other direction. If you haven't legalised your union, you may never discover the reason for this. Your Pisces simply becomes increasingly elusive and then disappears. You are left wondering what happened, but Pisces can't even explain the myriad feelings that led to the collapse, the paradise found and then lost.

Finishing with a Pisces is another matter. As the most open-ended sign of the zodiac, they don't really do closure. Nothing is cut and dried and their hooks can remain in you forever. Be prepared to face a tsunami of recriminations and regret, a guilt trip, a sacrifice to be made. It takes a lot for Pisces to heal from unrequited love, but they can do it just by falling in love again!

Piscean Elizabeth Taylor lived her life playing out love dramas – moving between love goddess and victim over and over again.

For some people, union to a Pisces does not feel 'real'. It exists in the ethers, cannot be translated into normal life. The Pisces partner can feel strangely absent even when present. Perhaps they are unable to strip the veils of illusion that cover their version of reality, cannot manage in the everyday world and the partner tires of carrying the can and constantly feeling as if they have not lived up to the impossible romantic dream. What seemed magical at first has lost its fairy dust.

DESTINY

The Tribe: Moving with the Shoal

Pisces loves to move with the shoal, hiding themselves with safety in numbers. The fish can so easily merge into the group, the team, the tribe – entering an existing mob and instantly recalibrating and co-ordinating as if it was always thus. It's quite a knack they have of being perfectly at home and mirroring the subtle signals you put out in your organisation or tribe. Pisces is the person who holds the emotional centre of the group, the one who understands where everyone is coming from and they can be a highly unifying force.

They particularly love to be part of something spiritual, creative or inspiring. They are great with causes, even lost causes! They may be attracted to or create a guru even if they are nowhere near an ashram; their tendency to idealise means that they blot out anything that doesn't fit with their vision of perfection.

As team leader they tend to let everyone do their own thing. Which means the group can descend into chaos as every person's wishes and needs diverts and dilutes the direction every time.

The lesson of discernment can come through their experience of being part of something that they feel they've got caught up in. The process of extrication is never easy for Pisces who is always thinking about the what ifs. However, being strong enough to stand alone can be a vital rite of passage for them.

Pisces can weave magic into other people's lives, hold the dream, even when someone has stopped believing. They can make an experience glamorous and divine – waving a magic wand and materialising something special out of nowhere. Their friendship and advice is of the most soulful quality, raising your awareness, giving you heart even when you have lost yours. They are the friend when you are in need, and they may also need you. A lot!

PISCES

ALTAR OBJECTS

Place some of these objects on your altar or carry them with you in actual or pictorial form.

*

CRYSTAL: blue lace agate, aquamarine, angelite

MINERAL/METAL: platinum

PISCES SYMBOLS: fish, Neptune, Poseidon

TAROT CARD: The Moon

ANGEL CARDS: Angel Barakiel, Archangel Sandalphon

FLOWERS: water lily, cosmos, narcissus

TREE: willow

SCENTS AND CANDLES: bergamot, white musk, frankincense

MEMORY BOARD/PHOTOGRAPHS/PICTURES: the sea, starfish; painting: 'Neptune and Amphitrite' by Paris Bordone

CLOTH: shimmering gauze, bejewelled velvet in colours of the sea

TALISMAN: mermaid, abalone shell

*

ACKNOWLEDGEMENTS

Dr Yubraj Sharma for being the master of the universe, all my amazing clients including the late Princess Diana for teaching me so much, Lindsey Evans, my brilliant Aries editor, for making this happen at the speed of light and Kate Miles, Sophie Elletson and Jessica Farrugia for their wonderful expertise. Warrior Queen Ileen Maizell, for sparking the idea and connection, and Taurean Titan Caroline de Wolfe, my agent. Also my soul sisters: Andrea, Jackie, Jacky, Julia and the Matrix posse, and my beautiful New York family of friends.

INDEX